Inflatables

DAG PIKE

D0544130

ADLARD COLES NAUTICAL
London

ACKNOWLEDGEMENTS

My grateful thanks to all the inflatable and RIB manufacturers who gave help, advice and photos so generously. Thanks also to the RNLI for introducing me to inflatable boats all those years ago and providing the experience and facilities for developing the early RIB.

Two people deserve special mention, Gina Haines my assistant for her work on the manuscript and index, and Carole Edwards for the sterling work of editing this book.

This edition published 1994 by Adlard Coles Nautical
an imprint of A & C Black (Publishers) Ltd
35 Bedford Row, London WC1R 4JH

Copyright © Dag Pike 1994

ISBN 0-7136-3881-8

Typeset in 10 on 12pt Palatino by Falcon Graphic Art Ltd
Printed and bound in Great Britain by
The Cromwell Press, Melksham, Wiltshire

Apart from any fair dealing for the purposes of research or private study, or criticism or review, as permitted under the Copyright, Design and Patents Act, 1988, this publication may be reproduced, stored or transmitted, in any form or by any means, only with the prior permission in writing of the publishers, or in the case of reprographic reproduction in accordance with the terms of licences issued by the Copyright Licensing Agency. Inquiries concerning reproduction outside those terms should be sent to the publishers at the address above.

A CIP catalogue record for this book is available from the British Library.

CONTENTS

CHAPTER 1

SUCCESS STORY

Inflatables are remarkable boats; they range in size from tiny yacht tenders to massive 50 footers and are found operating in sheltered harbours and in the roughest seas. Probably among the most versatile boats afloat, they are used by beginners and the hardiest of professionals, and are found all over the world. This widespread acceptance of the inflatable hides the fact that the simple inflatable boat has a history going back little more than 60 years whilst the rigid inflatable is only half that age. In a few short years, in terms of maritime history, inflatables have changed the face of boating.

Folding boats

What is it that makes the inflatable so successful? There are many reasons and these have changed with time. Initially, the idea of having a boat which could be packed into a small space and inflated when required for use was the primary requirement. There are a great many patents for boats which can be folded up for stowage, but the inflatable is the most logical folding boat there is.

Yacht tenders and some of the smaller inflatables are still designed to be transported folded up. A boat which can be carried in the boot of a car has its attractions and one which can be stowed in a locker on board saves the worry of having the dinghy on deck or being towed astern. But in practice it seems that inflatables are much more likely to be transported on the roof of a car in their inflated state than in the boot, deflated. Yachtsmen prefer to tow their inflatables rather than deflate them for stowage on board. People prefer not to have to go through the chore of inflation and deflation so the boats stay inflated as far as possible.

So whilst the ability to deflate the boat and pack it away will appeal to some owners, this is obviously not the main reason for the popularity of inflatables. The development of the rigid inflatable made this clear, because whilst you can reduce the beam of these boats by deflating them, they certainly won't fold away into a compact stowage. To find the attraction of the inflatable we must look at some of its other attributes to find the answer; one of these has to be the built-in fender.

Water skiing can be very practical from even a small inflatable or RIB. Here a 40 hp outboard provides adequate power for the job but an engine of half that power can be used on the smallest boats. *Photo: Avon.*

Damage limitation

A built-in fender is one of the factors which makes the inflatable such a practical boat. You can leave it alongside the gleaming topsides of a yacht and be confident that it won't damage the shiny surface. The inflatable makes an excellent rescue boat because you can go alongside another craft in the open sea with little fear of damage to either craft. For the diver or fisherman the inflatable can nose between rocks or be dragged on to inaccessible beaches. It is a go-anywhere boat which provides a very practical solution to many boating problems.

Whilst this practicality and go-anywhere capability applies to the inflatable boat, it doesn't account for the widespread use of the rigid inflatable. It seemed like a retrograde step to develop a concept which combined the rigid sections of conventional boats and the inflatable sections of inflatable boats. It could be argued that this was getting the worst of both worlds, the maintenance problems of the inflatable tube, and the lack of resilience and fendering of the rigid hull. However, it did have very practical applications.

Rigid hulls

The original rigid inflatable was developed in order to reduce wear and tear on the fabric bottom of inflatable boats when they were dragged across beaches. Abrasive sand and stones are not very kind to the bottom fabric of the inflatable and in the days when I worked for the RNLI, maintaining their fleet of over 100 rescue boats, damage to the bottom fabric was a major maintenance problem. Most of the abrasions were towards the back end of the boat, so we tried replacing this rear section of the floor with plywood. This prototype 'half' rigid inflatable worked, up to a point, but did tend to move the wear and tear problem further forward!

Eventually, the whole fabric floor was replaced with plywood, shaped as far as possible to replicate the bottom shape of the inflatable. Again, it worked, but it was far from ideal. However, by using a rigid hull, the way was open to design underwater hull shapes which couldn't be achieved with the pure inflatable as the supporting rigid floors and keel air tubes tended to limit shapes which were practical. It took 10 prototypes before the logical underwater shape for the rigid inflatable was found. This proved to be the deep-vee hull which was then gaining popularity in the sports boat market.

The combination of the rigid deep-vee hull and the inflatable tube produced a boat which was dramatic in terms of its seaworthiness and performance in rough seas. The inflatable had proved itself a remarkable craft in operating in surf and rough sea conditions on rescue work, but it gave a rough ride with violent slamming motions, largely due to the relatively flat bottom of the boat. The deep-vee rigid inflatable gave a much more comfortable ride, as the hull shape cushioned the impact with waves whilst the inflatable topsides still provided the important fendering when going alongside.

That Atlantic 21, which was developed as the first rigid inflatable rescue boat, was one of the most seaworthy boats ever built and it remains so today. What proved impressive was that in open sea waves and in surf it could out-perform any conventional rigid hulled boat of the same or even larger sizes. This fact made us stop, think and analyse the performance of the boat very critically to find out why it was so good.

An impressive performance

In analysing the performance of the rigid inflatable there were a number of reasons why it was better than conventional rigid hulled boats. Probably the most important feature is the role which the tube plays in the performance of both inflatables and RIBs. When an inflatable boat goes alongside a jetty or another craft, the inflatable tube will deform to absorb the impact which is more gradual and is partially absorbed by the cushioning effect of the air tube. Now consider what happens in waves. The deep vee hull will absorb the initial shock of re-entry and reduce the slamming, but the inflatable tube creates a further shock absorbing surface so that the ride becomes smoother and less physically stressful. On a rigid boat, the hull cannot 'give' when hit by a wave and it is only the smooth hull lines which can help to absorb the wave impact.

With an inflatable tube, the tube itself will change shape under wave impact and so you have what could be termed a 'variable geometry' hull which will change shape automatically to match the wave conditions.

Instead of a wave hitting hard on the hull, the hull itself will momentarily change shape thereby helping to absorb the impact and smooth the water flow. The variable geometry hull concept applies equally to inflatables as well as to rigid inflatables and is the secret behind much of the superior performance characteristics of these craft.

There were other characteristics of the new generation of rigid inflatable boats (RIBs) which helped to make it superior to anything which had gone before. These first RIBs had only a minimal transom and the deck level was above the waterline. This meant that any water which came on board, drained out through the stern immediately. This characteristic meant that the boat could be driven with a degree of impunity in surf and similar conditions without any real worry about water coming on board and having to be pumped out.

Another factor, is the driving position. The saddle seat, now familiar on rigid inflatables, was developed for the early prototypes. It provides a much more positive means of controlling the boat than alternative forms of seating. The motion of a RIB at sea is very much like that of a horse where the saddle has proved so effective. The saddle provides grip and security and leaves both hands free, so that the wheel and throttle can be used effectively to control the boat.

So the superb performance of the RIB is, to a certain extent, due to a combination of the variable geometry of the inflatable tube and a driving position which leaves you in full control of the boat. Later chapters will cover these variable geometry and control concepts in more detail, but they are the vital elements which have made the rigid inflatable the most seaworthy craft of its size anywhere in the world.

Tough in the extreme

One of the definitions of a rescue boat is that it can go to sea in bad conditions and not only survive, but be effective enough to go to the aid of casualties. Both inflatables and RIBs can meet this requirement, and this gives a large safety margin to both pleasure and professional users.

Both inflatables and RIBs are now widely used by professionals. Navies around the world now carry RIBs on board as a highly practical 'sea boat' which can be used for a whole host of duties. Police, customs and coastguards use them for patrol and enforcement whilst they are widely used in the offshore oil industry for rescue and routine duties. The inflatable provides a very effective boarding boat when transfers have to be made in the open sea.

Exploration and adventure are further areas where inflatables and RIBs are well suited. From the Arctic to the Tropics, these boats can provide water transport and support in most environments. The inflatable can be the ideal form of transport in shallow tropical rivers, but it is equally useful amongst ice floes. It is this use of inflatables and RIBs in extreme conditions and by professional users which gives the leisure user great confidence. Here is the type of boat which doesn't have to be nursed or

The current designs of inflatables are stylish enough to appeal to sports boat buyers and they are ideal for reaching remote beaches. *Photo: Novamarine.*

pampered, which will stand up to rough use. The leisure user is unlikely to push his boat anywhere near the limits as the professional might, but it's nice to know that the reserves are there if the going gets tough. The other attraction for the leisure user, of course, is that the professional role of the inflatable or rigid inflatable gives it credibility in the eyes of the onlooker and it looks at home at the pontoon of the smartest yacht club.

Tube materials

Part of the success of the inflatable boat has come about from the development of new materials. The concept of using inflatable containers to provide buoyancy goes back to the use of animal skins over 2000 years ago. These tended to have a short life and reliability was not good. Even when inflatable tubes were constructed from rubber-proofed fabrics, the materials and adhesives were still the weak point. The Mackintosh raincoat company made one of the first inflatable boats for an Arctic expedition around 150 years ago. The French company Zodiac and the British company RFD were amongst the pioneers, and the early boats used a cotton fabric impregnated with natural rubber.

These early fabrics were prone to rot and perishing and the boats needed great care to prevent deterioration. The armed forces commissioned inflatable boats built for specialised use during World War II and with the rubber shortage, types of synthetic rubber were developed and these, combined with man-made fibres such as nylon, led to a new generation of materials for inflatable boats. This started to make them a viable proposition for a much wider market.

Today, the science and technology of both the inflatable boat fabric and the adhesives used to glue them, has developed products which give the boats a reliability and performance which matches that of rigid hulled boats. Even so, the development of the inflatable boat has been a painful process with problems such as wicking and porosity to overcome. Users can now be confident, however, that the basic problems of the construction of inflatables and rigid inflatables have been overcome. Inflatable products can now be produced reliably provided that the manufacture sticks to accepted practices. This may lead to a general conformity about the way boats are put together but it still leaves a wide range of different design concepts where individual ideas can be developed.

New materials such as PVC and polyurethane materials are now being used for smaller boats and this is opening up the possibility of using high frequency welding rather than adhesives for building boats. This in turn could open up the way to industrial manufacturing processes rather than the largely hand built methods which are used today.

Foam tube boats and other developments

Many rigid inflatables, particularly in the larger sizes, now use tubes which are partially or fully filled with foam. These tubes are much firmer than the inflatable tube with virtually no give under the influence of wave impact. The Americans call them 'bumper boats' which tends to sum up their role; in these boats the tube section of the boat is used almost entirely as a fender. There is a loss of the variable geometry characteristics of the inflatable tube, but these boats are another variation on the rigid inflatable theme and their place in the inflatable world has to be recognised, and their merits discussed.

Perhaps one of the greatest tributes to the inflatable is the development of boats which, at first glance look almost exactly like an inflatable, but which are in fact moulded entirely from GRP or built from aluminium. Here boat builders are trying to cash in on the appeal of the inflatable and suggest that, because of the wear and tear to which an inflatable can be prone, why not have the same shape, but in a more hard wearing material? What such boat builders fail to appreciate is that it is the very flexibility of the inflatable which endows it with its better characteristics, and that the shape is far from ideal if you are going to use GRP as the only building material.

The inflatable market also has upgrading potential. At least one enterprising builder is, at present, offering to convert inflatables into rigid inflatables by inserting a GRP hull. The variety of possibilities in the inflatable and RIB market also extends to the propulsion systems where, in addition to the traditional outboards, inboard petrol and diesel engines are now being used, to power stern drives, water jets and even surface-piercing propellers.

The scope of the rigid inflatable has also widened considerably. The first pilot boats to use the RIB concept, although with a foam rather than inflatable tube, are in use. The first 100 mph rigid inflatable, powered by twin diesels of 1800 hp is currently opening up new markets in the fast patrol boat arena. Rigid inflatables with wheelhouses are now common as is the self-righting RIB. Most of these developments have taken place in the commercial or professional side of the market, but experience has shown that developments here generally filter into the leisure market.

RIB racing is a fast-growing sport with an enthusiastic following. Part of its appeal is the ease of transportation to race venues and the challenge of pushing these responsive craft to their limit. *Photo: Delta.*

The leisure side has made its own developments. The flying rigid inflatable, which uses a wing and a power unit rather like a microlight aircraft, is up and flying; this perhaps gives the ultimate in flexible operations. There are inflatable hovercraft operating, and of course there are sailing inflatables. The pure inflatable may have got left a little behind in the race to develop the RIB, but modern versions are used in large numbers in the leisure market where simplicity and low price are the important criteria. The folding characteristics of the inflatable are still used by the military, and inflatable boats are a serious part of the modern lifesaving equipment on many classes of sea-going ships.

The market for inflatables and RIBs is enormous. There are probably over a million of these boats around the world and the number continues to grow. The number of manufacturers also continues to grow, and unlike the mainstream boat building industry, where production tends to be concentrated in larger units, the inflatable boat industry is constantly adding new builders to its list. There are the major manufacturers such as Zodiac and Avon, but there are literally hundreds of smaller builders. For instance in Argentina there are 12 builders of inflatables and RIBs, whilst Italy boasts over 50.

The inflatable boat is now a widely accepted part of the maritime scene. This is due largely to the early pioneers who persevered with the development despite considerable difficulties. Now there is a need to promote the use, maintenance and servicing of this unique class of boat. This is the aim of this book, which brings over 30 years of experience in the design and maintenance of these boats to explain how and why they work so well and how both professionals and amateurs alike can get the best out of their inflatable and rigid inflatable boats.

CHAPTER 2

INFLATABLE DESIGN AND DEVELOPMENT

There are three main hull shapes for inflatable boats. The yacht tender type of inflatable has the inflatable tube going right round the boat and there is no transom used and, generally speaking, no rigid floor. This is probably the simplest and the most basic inflatable boat. The second type, which generally operates at higher speeds, has a transom and rigid or semi-rigid floor boards inserted into the hull to give and maintain its shape. The third type encompasses all those not included in the first two categories; it can include canoes and kayaks, inflatable boats which have an inflatable floor, catamarans and the sea sled type of inflatable which is designed to be towed behind another vessel and is really just a fun craft. The inflatable air tube is the common factor in all these designs but let us look at each concept individually to see how it is put together and constructed, and from this you will start to get a better understanding of inflatable boats and also an idea of what will meet your requirements.

Dinghy inflatables

This type of inflatable has tended to become a modern replacement for the traditional wood or fibreglass dinghy. Although the dinghy concept could include those inflatables which have a transom but are designed for low speed, those will be included in the next section. Here we are talking about inflatables which have the tube going all round the boat. The primary advantage of this type of dinghy inflatable is that it is completely made from fabric with the only hard parts in the design being a few of the fittings. This makes it light and easy to stow in a small space. Also, there is probably more usable room inside the boat than in a comparable-sized transom boat. Against this has to be weighed the disadvantage that with no rigid members in the boat, it tends to be floppy if it gets soft. It is not always the easiest boat to control, and it is virtually impossible to remove all the water that collects in the bottom of the boat, so that people and luggage invariably get wet in these boats. However, they are extremely practical craft and, in addition to their role as yacht tenders, they can also be used individually for such purposes as fishing on calm waters. Judging by the numbers which are sold, they make one of the most popular yacht tenders on the market today.

An inflatable floor improves the rigidity of the whole boat and still allows quick and easy assembly.

An inflatable tube can only be made in straight lines, so if you want to produce a boat shape, you have to construct it with angular corners. For these dinghy inflatables, the bow is pointed by incorporating a couple of these angled corners into the shape to make it reasonably boat-shaped. The sides are made parallel and at the stern there is usually a single angled segment to give the effect of a partially rounded shape. To help maintain the shape of the boat there is usually a cross-inflatable tube somewhere

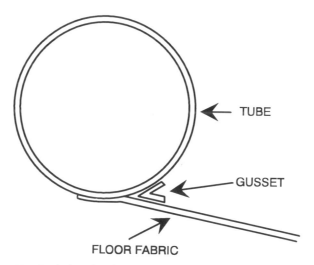

The method used to attach the tube of an inflatable to the floor. The inside gusset is essential to prevent the floor peeling off and it also serves as a resting point for the wooden floor.

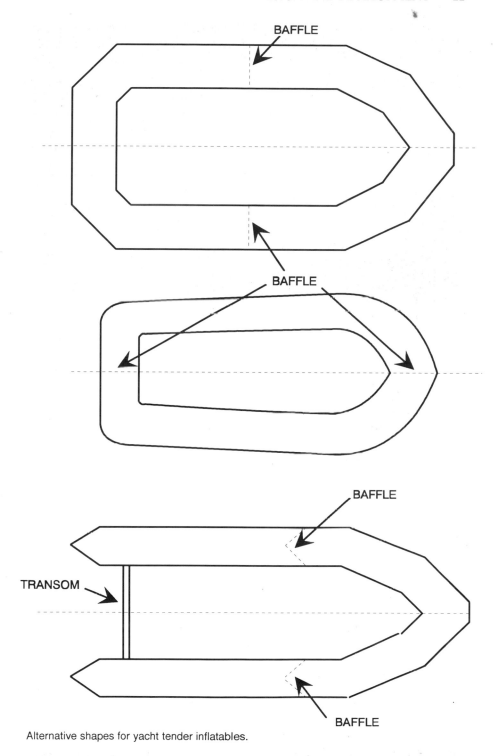

Alternative shapes for yacht tender inflatables.

near amidships. This cross tube is usually independent and removable from the boat and it serves not only to keep the boat in shape, but also as a seat for rowing. The bow sections, in addition to being angled inward to give a boat-like shape, are usually angled slightly upward as well to help increase the freeboard of the bow and reduce the chance of shipping water when the boat is loaded. To complete the picture, the fabric floor is simply glued to the bottom of the tubes all round and there you have the most basic of inflatable boats.

To make this type of boat safer, the inflatable tubes are normally divided into at least two individual compartments with baffles inside the tubes. This means that if one section of the boat gets punctured, at least the remaining half stays inflated and this is usually enough to support the occupants and cargo in an emergency. These baffles are vital to safety and an inflatable boat which only has single compartment tubes should not be considered a viable proposition. The baffles are normally amidships on each side and correspond roughly with the location of the cross-tube, so that if one half doesn't inflate you still have a structure which is surrounded by an air tube, and if you pull the deflated section up and over, then at least you have some sort of flotation device to keep you safe until rescue comes.

The baffles installed to isolate the compartment are usually conical or hemispherical in shape and reversible. This means that the cone will extend into the compartment which has the lower pressure. Because they are reversible it doesn't matter in what order compartments are inflated and, in addition to their isolation function, they also help to equalize the inevitably different pressures which occur in adjacent compartments.

On some models of inflatable, the cross tube may be replaced by a rigid thwart which is attached to the top of the tube. This makes a more solid base for a seat and it also creates a firm step when boarding the boat. However, this rigid thwart does not allow the boat to be folded into such a compact package. A lifeline or grabline is usually fitted on the side of the

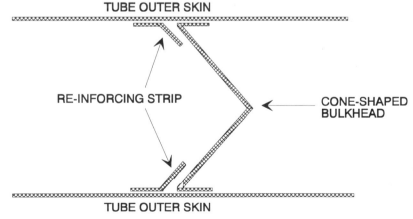

The installation of a baffle inside an air tube. The reinforcing strip is essential to make sure that the air pressure does not peel the baffle away and also makes the baffle reversible so that it can adjust to varying air pressure on either side.

tubes, at least in the midships areas, but these may be replaced with rigid handholds which make it easier to carry the boat up and down the beach or on to a jetty. A painter is attached to a ring at the bow and an optional extra is a bow dodger which can be clipped into place to give protection to the occupants or cargo in the front of the boat.

Propulsion of these boats is either by oars or small outboard motor, normally 2 or 3 hp petrol-driven two-strokes. For rowing, the cross inflatable tube or thwart acts as the seat; this is usually fixed in place by a couple of clips attached to loops or permanently glued in place so that it doesn't move under the pressure of rowing. Rowlocks can be either of the moulded rubber type, which tend to reduce the chance of chafe when the boat is rolled up, or the more conventional type of rowlock which fits into a moulded fitting attached to the top of the tube. For powering this type of inflatable with an outboard motor, a metal frame is hung over the air tube at the stern of the boat. This sits in moulded rubber brackets; the metal frame is fitted with a wooden engine mount to which the outboard motor is clamped. For the low horsepower engines for which these inflatables are designed, this type of bracket is quite adequate, but the thrust of the outboard below the waterline does create a twisting moment on the rear tubes and this has to be resisted by rigidity in the main inflatable structure of the boat. Too much power from the outboard can cause the tube to kink and bend and some of the more powerful outboards of say 4 or 5 hp need to be used with care on this type of dinghy inflatable.

Some dinghy inflatables are fitted with a slatted wooden or GRP floor which can give a drier surface for standing on, but also helps to maintain the shape of the boat. However, this type of addition does reduce the simplicity of the craft. Many manufacturers of these simple inflatables offer a variety of optional equipment including alternative seats and floors so that the boat can be equipped to meet specific requirements.

An alternative type of dinghy inflatable is one which is built in an oval shape. This type is found at the cheap end of the inflatable market and they tend to be constructed from polyurethane or PVC. They are made by simply cutting out two oval shapes from the fabric which are then heat- or high-frequency welded together; a floor is attached which can also be inflatable. There are no baffles fitted and these boats tend to be very basic, their attraction being the bright colours rather than their construction and they tend to be aimed at the fun market rather than for hard practical use.

Sports inflatables

The sports inflatable comprises a U-shaped tube with the transom mounted across the two arms of the U. The transom is glued in place and the fabric floor is mounted around the tube and on to the transom, so completing the basic boat structure. A rigid floor is then inserted inside the boat to help maintain its shape, and between this rigid floor and the fabric bottom of the boat there is usually a wooden or inflatable keel fitted in order to shape the bottom of the boat into a slight vee. This vee tends to be more pronounced at the bow and is probably no more than 5° at the transom, but this serves to improve directional stability and to cushion the ride to a certain extent. The keel member is probably better as an inflatable tube than constructed in wood because it creates a more sympathetic rounded shape to the fabric floor. It also removes hard spots and this in turn reduces the chafe which is inevitable between the rigid and inflatable members of a boat. Use of this keel, whether inflatable or wood serves to tension the floor fabric and this helps to create a reasonably efficient planing surface.

The main inflatable tube around the boat is divided into compartments. Whilst on smaller boats it would be simple just to incorporate two compartments, by having a single baffle at the bow, this wouldn't provide adequate security in the event of a puncture, so the normal practice is to have baffles towards the front end of the side air tubes which, on smaller boats, effectively divides the air tube into three compartments. Loss of any one of these might reduce the boat's performance but it enables the basic shape of the boat to be retained intact, and it should be possible to make progress at slow speed at least to get safely into harbour. Larger sports inflatables of this type will have each side tube divided into two compartments and with this type of division, loss of any one of the side compartments will not have a tremendous effect on the performance of the boat.

The transom is not mounted right at the stern of the boat; it is usually up to half a metre in from the extremity of the tubes. This offers protection for the outboard motor or a stern drive leg but equally it means that if the bow of the boat lifts unduly to a wave or under the thrust of the motor, these tube extensions provide a reaction against that thrust and serve to help keep the boat running level. The treatment for the end of the side inflatable tubes varies with the manufacturer but the general trend is to create a cone shape terminating in a moulded rubber fitting at the apex of the cone. This is the simplest shape to manufacture in the fabric but an alternative is rounded and almost hemispherical, but it is not easy to get tidy seams in the fabric with this type of shape. Another alternative is to use a moulded rubber insert to seal the end of the tube, and this can be either mounted vertically or, as one manufacturer does, mounted at an angle to effectively extend the waterline length of the boat. At the rear end of the main tube, there is usually a small wedge shape section inserted round the tube at the bottom which helps to peel away the water cleanly thereby reducing the friction drag on the hull and improving performance.

The floors which give the boat rigidity and help to maintain its shape are usually fitted in two or three sections so that their size conforms roughly with the size of the boat when it is folded up. These floors are provided with continuity by having side members which clip along the sides of the floor sections and fit under the inflatable tube in the angle where this meets the fabric floor. The whole floor structure is locked together with these longitudinal stringers on each side. At the transom, the floor butts against the lower edge of the transom to help take the thrust of the outboard motor whilst at the forward end there is usually a thrust board permanently glued into the vee of the bow of the boat; this helps to

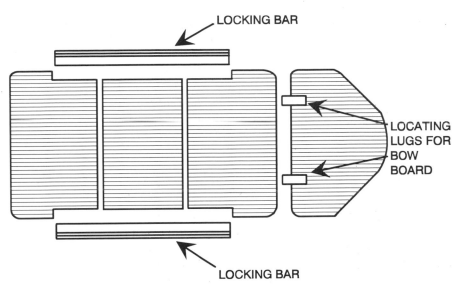

Typical floorboard arrangement for a small inflatable. It is the side stringers which lock the boards together whilst the lugs on the bow section allow a degree of flexibility at this end of the boat.

transmit forward thrust right throughout the inflatable structure. Many modern boats use GRP mouldings for the rigid sections of the floor because these have reduced maintenance and are usually lighter than the plywood alternative. Aluminium is another possibility where light weight is required. The matching of the bending characteristics of the floor and those of the inflatable boat is quite important to produce an integrated boat hull which will flex to a certain degree without overstressing any of the individual members. The inflatable tubes themselves have a surprising degree of rigidity when they are inflated to the 3 psi which is used on most modern designs. This relatively high inflation pressure in the main air tubes helps to reduce the stresses and strains on the rigid floor members which can still flex to a degree at the transom and where the floor boards meet at the bow thrust board. The longitudinal stringers of the floor are often built to allow a degree of flexibility.

The high pressures used in the inflatable tubes of modern inflatables does help to improve both the performance and the rigidity of the boat but it also serves to make the inflatable more bouncy and an inflation pressure of 2 psi will give a more comfortable ride. On most boats there is a degree of flexibility in the design; the manufacturers recognise that they have little control over the inflation pressure at which the boat may be operated and that this can vary from day to day. The boat therefore has to be able to accommodate a considerable range of inflation pressures and still perform satisfactorily.

A bow dodger is usually fitted to these boats to offer protection and normally this is permanently glued in place. The bow dodger can terminate in a flexible windscreen mounted around its aft edge to give further protection to the occupants and these sports inflatables are generally much more sophisticated than the dinghy types. Rowlocks for rowing will normally be fitted on the top of the tube to provide an auxiliary means of propulsion and oars may be permanently mounted on these rowlocks, remaining stowed along the top of the tube ready for use. Alternatively, paddles can be fitted into fabric sockets fitted inside the tubes as an emergency means of propulsion but anyone who has tried to propel an inflatable for any distance with paddles will know that they are not very effective. Another useful fitting which is permanently fitted into most boats is a storage pouch under the forward canopy for stowing equipment such as flares, anchor, engine tools and spares and other emergency equipment. Rubbing strips will be fitted in areas where the manufacturers expect wear particularly around the outside of the boat and at the bow.

Smaller types of sports inflatables will normally use engines with tiller steering and manual starting so that the whole installation is simple and straightforward. A mattress may be fitted on to the bottom floorboards to provide a cushioned base for the crew, and the air tubes themselves can be used as seating. This type of basic layout is suitable even for inflatables up to 5 metres in length but often with sports inflatables over 4 metres proper seating is provided combined with a steering wheel and remote throttle and gear control. In most cases these are options which the manufacturer can supply, enabling an owner to outfit the boat to the level of sophistication he needs.

In talking about designs here we have tended to concentrate on those developed for the leisure market. For professional use in the rescue, military and safety markets, the same basic designs are used but the accent tends to be towards a much more rugged craft. The leisure market is price sensitive and so manufacturers tend to be looking for the most cost-effective solutions to the design and construction of the boat. For professional use, it is quality that counts and the difference between the two types of craft is less one of basic design and more in the quality of the materials and fittings which are used. Heavier duty fendering will almost certainly be used and possibly even a stronger grade of fabric. The aim is to make the boats generally tougher to withstand hard use and many items of specialised equipment may also be fitted.

Alternative inflatables

The alternative types of inflatables are usually built for specific applications. However, mention should be made of inflatables of the sports boat type which have fully inflated floors. There is certainly attraction in this configuration because it means that apart from the transom there are no rigid members in the boat, so it gets more benefit from the cushioning and impact absorbing qualities of the inflatable structure. The inflatable floors of these boats usually comprise a series of parallel tubes perhaps 15 cm in diameter linked together longitudinally along the bottom of the boat. When inflated hard, these tubes provide a rigid base for the boat which is generally stable enough to act as a planing surface, certainly at moderate speeds. The main drawback of this type of inflatable is the considerable extra resistance created by the inflatable tubes and the less than efficient planing surface; so, for a given power, these boats don't usually perform quite so well as those of more conventional design. The boats are also more complex to manufacture and the inflatable floor does not cope so readily with being dragged across a beach. Another snag is that the bottom of the boat is virtually flat and doesn't have the same cushioning effect of a shallow vee bottom. However, for those who want an inflatable of the sports type which can be made ready for use simply by inflation, this concept has its attractions.

Other types of more specialised inflatables are those of the canoe or kayak type which, because of their foldable nature, can be attractive when trying to reach remote locations with a canoe. Apart from a rigid seat, these canoes and kayaks are usually completely inflatable but in order to maintain adequate rigidity they are usually inflated to fairly high pressures. The inflatable structure usually comprises two or more tubes on each side linked by a fabric floor, but manufacturers have created a great variety of different concepts to choose from.

Another specialised type of inflatable is the river raft or river runner which is specifically designed for negotiating the rapids and torrents of white water rivers. They are only designed for a one way trip down the river and propulsion is limited usually to paddles or oars whose function is for steering rather than propulsion. In design, these river rafts are like a larger version of a dinghy inflatable with no rigid members incorporated; when negotiating violent rapids, the inflatable structure will bend and

River rafting with a purpose designed Avon inflatable.

twist to conform to the water surface. The use of inflatable structures for this arduous sport demonstrates the capability of an inflatable boat, not only to maintain buoyancy and stability in these extreme conditions, but also to cope with abrasion on rocks and rough beaches. Heavy duty fabric floors are fitted to these boats to improve abrasion resistance and they also have a basic type of self-draining system through the sides of the fabric floor. These river runners can vary in size from 5 metres up to 10 metres and they are a specialised part of the inflatable market.

There is considerable logic in the catamaran type of inflatable, mainly because it uses straight tubes which require no careful design and shaping and no complex assembly. One catamaran concept, designed for commercial operations in the USA, uses straight, large diameter inflatable tubes matched to an aluminium cross deck in order to create a cargo platform for transporting vehicles or cargo along rivers or across relatively calm stretches of water. Catamaran designs have also been used for racing inflatables and one or two manufacturers use what is essentially a catamaran hull but with the fabric floor stretched across between the two tubes to create the underwater surface. Some designs of this type have a small rigid transom at the bow to help maintain the shape and make construction simple. There is a wide variety of options within the twin tube type of inflatable whilst there are many possibilities for catamaran hull inflatables to be used for specialised applications. These more specialised designs tend to have features which can be attractive for particular applications, but the general trend in sportsboat inflatable design is towards those using the U-shaped tube.

Fabrics and adhesives

The key to the modern inflatable is the fabric from which it is constructed and the adhesives used to join the fabrics. The earlier fabrics made from cotton and natural rubber had a very short lifespan unless they were very carefully looked after and also had limited strength. It is only when new synthetic materials became available that the inflatable became a viable proposition. Today there are three components incorporated into modern inflatable boat fabrics, and these are the interior reinforcing material which gives the fabric its strength and stretch characteristics, the main air sealing rubber skin, and a second abrasion resistant skin. The second and third components of the fabric may be combined in one coating.

REINFORCING FABRICS
The reinforcing fabric, which was originally cotton, may now be either nylon, polyester or Kevlar. Nylon is by far the most popular fabric in use today as the base fabric for inflatable boat manufacture. It has high strength and its stretch capability can accommodate the often complex shapes required in the construction of inflatable boats. However this stretching makes designing more difficult because the designer has to take it into account when working out the dimensions of the tube. Experience

solves this problem and nylon makes a very practical and comparatively cheap base fabric. Unlike nylon, polyester has little stretch and so much more precise assembly of the inflatable parts is required. It is mostly used for boats where the seams are heat welded or vulcanised rather than glued because it has a higher melting point than nylon.

Kevlar is an excellent material as a base fabric for inflatable boat construction because of its very high strength characteristics and its stretch is comparable to nylon. Boats constructed with a Kevlar base fabric can be inflated to much higher pressures than those using other fabrics (up to 5 psi) but Kevlar is also expensive. Its use as a base fabric tends to be limited to specialised applications such as military craft where weight is important and the high strength of the Kevlar allows a lower weight of fabric to be used. Another specialised application might be where extra rigidity is required; the higher inflation pressures achieved with Kevlar fabrics allow firmer tubes. Again the main application here could be in the military market where a boat is required to be completely made from inflatable or fabric materials but still be capable of relatively high planing speeds which in turn demands a higher rigidity from the inflatable tubes.

COATING MATERIALS

The base material provides the strength for the inflatable tube fabric but it is the coating that provides the air tightness. The fabric is coated on both sides and this coating not only has to be capable of preventing the air in the tube from escaping, but also has to be abrasion resistant as well as resistant to attack from battery acid, engine fuels and oils and the effects of ultra violet light. Ultra violet light in particular can have a strong influence on many rubbers and the two main synthetic rubbers used in inflatable boat manufacture, neoprene and hypalon are reasonably immune to this. Of these two rubbers, hypalon has marginally better characteristics in terms of abrasion resistance and resistance to chemicals and sunlight and to a large degree they are virtually indestructible. Hypalon tends to be a more difficult rubber to glue but with modern adhesives this is not a major problem. Hypalon is the favoured proofing used for the outside skin of inflatable boat fabric but this is largely a question of its cosmetic appeal. Hypalon has a better surface finish than neoprene, being smoother, slightly shiny and easier to clean. It is also available in a wider range of colours.

Different manufacturers have a varying approach to the fabric they use but in one way or another almost all of them use proofing materials which are either hypalon only or a combination of neoprene and hypalon. In some cases, the neoprene will be applied to the base fabric first and a separate coating of hypalon placed on top. In others the neoprene and the hypalon will be mixed together in various proportions and this combination rubber will be applied to the base fabric. Alternatively, neoprene may be used as the inside coating and hypalon on the outside. Most inflatable boat builders will buy their fabric from specialised fabric manufacturers and only a very few of the largest builders produce their own fabric and

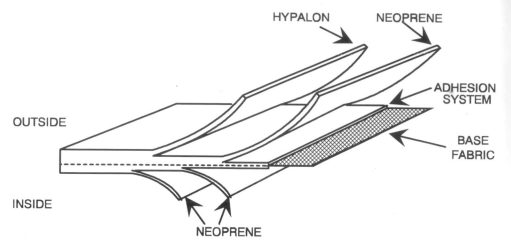

The fabric from which inflatables are made comprises several layers. Hypalon makes an effective outer covering because of its toughness and resistance to chemicals and ultra violet light.

have full control over the specification. Most builders have their own favoured type of fabric with particular combinations of neoprene and hypalon which they feel is best suited for the job, together with an adhesive which, in their view, will provide the strongest joints. While it is virtually impossible for an inflatable boat buyer to assess the merits of particular combinations, the best gauge of the builder's confidence in his material and adhesives, is the length of time he is prepared to guarantee the boat. This is your best guide to quality, although this obviously has to be weighed against cost.

ADHESIVES
As with fabrics, adhesive manufacturers have differing formulations. The two main categories of adhesives are those which are a single part adhesive and can be used directly from the tube or tin and the two-part adhesives where the two parts have to be mixed together in carefully controlled proportions before use. The inflatable boat builders almost invariably use the two part adhesive because of its far superior characteristics. Single part adhesives tend to be restricted to the repair kits which are supplied with inflatable boats. Here, ease of use and the ability to use just a small amount of the adhesive in a particular can or tube as required without compromising the remainder can be an overriding requirement when it comes to selecting a suitable adhesive.

One of the most popular adhesives used in the manufacture of inflatable boats is Boscoprene 2404 which is a two-part adhesive. This adhesive has a limited shelf life and once the two parts are mixed, the adhesive has to be used within an hour or two after which it is unfit for further use. Whilst it might be attractive from a repair point of view to think you can use just a small proportion from each of the two components, these have to be mixed in very precise amounts and this precise mixing can only be achieved by using the whole amount in each container. For the boat builder who uses large amounts of adhesive this is not a serious problem, provided he uses strict quality control. For repair work the same two-part adhesive is by far the best and it is available in relatively small quantities, but any left over has to be thrown away. The single part adhesive tends to provide a more practical solution for repair work provided great care is taken in the way the repair is done and the conditions under which they are done (see Chapter 10). The fact that manufacturers always use two-part adhesives will indicate that there is a considerable difference between the capabilities of the two adhesives.

PLASTICS

Alternative materials for inflatable boat building are the plastics PVC and polyurethane. Both are probably as impregnable to deterioration and are as abrasion resistant as hypalon but they are less easy to glue; heat or high frequency welding is an alternative means of joining these materials. PVC fabric comes in two forms, one which is unreinforced and is pure PVC sheeting and the other which is reinforced in the same way as the rubber fabrics, with nylon being the primary backing material. Polyurethane is only used in the reinforced state with nylon or polyester being the backing material. Unreinforced PVC is cheap and easy to work but it will stretch considerably and obviously if stretched too much, the inflatable tube made of this material will burst. Unreinforced PVC is generally used for very small, cheap inflatable boats which are little larger than inflatable mattresses and are really childrens' play boats rather than serious inflatables. The stretching to which this material is prone means that these boats readily distort but the advantage of this material is that it can be easily heat welded and therefore lends itself to automated manufacturing processes and cheap production.

Reinforced PVC and polyurethane are materials with which many manufacturers are experimenting because of its capability of being heat or high frequency welded. Welding can be very effective and is certainly quicker, cleaner, cheaper and easier to automate than construction methods using adhesives, particularly when the high frequency techniques are used. The problem with using welding techniques on inflatable products is that the final seams have to be on the outside because that is the only position in which they can be sealed; it therefore requires clever and careful design in order to achieve a satisfactory finished product. However, the heat or high frequency welding techniques lend themselves to more automated production methods and several builders are working on ways to use these materials for their ranges of production boats. For smaller inflatables, PVC and polyurethane is already being used and this trend is likely to spread. These materials may reduce the initial price of inflatables, but problems may be found when repairs are necessary because of the difficulty in gluing these fabrics. However, when a problem like this arises, a new type of adhesive tends to be formulated to solve it.

APPLYING THE COATINGS

To manufacture unreinforced PVC sheeting, the raw material is passed through rollers to achieve the desired thickness of film but with reinforced fabrics there are two main techniques which are used for coating the base fabric with the rubber compound. The first of these is called 'knifing'. Here the fabric is passed under a straight or knife edge which stretches the full width of fabric; the coating rubber is forced down behind this edge so that the knife spreads the coating evenly over the fabric. Each side is done alternately and more than one layer can be added if necessary with this process.

The problem with knifing is that it doesn't necessarily provide a good bond between the base fabric and the rubber and there have been many cases of delamination with material made by this process. A much better process for making the rubber fabric, and one used for virtually all modern fabrics, is 'calendaring'; here the fabric, together with the coating rubber compound, is passed between rollers at a carefully measured distance apart. By passing the fabric and coating through the rollers, the coating is firmly impregnated into the fabric and a very positive bond results. Calendaring is very much the preferred process but the machinery required is more expensive than with knifing; it is worth checking when you buy a boat which process is used for manufacturing the fabric.

Where the first coat on the fabric is neoprene followed by a second coat of hypalon, the material has to go through the calendaring process twice. One problem with adding neoprene in this way is that the bond between the neoprene and its hypalon coating is not always as positive as it could be. Mixing the two rubber compounds together at the calendaring stage seems to be the preferred method but different manufacturers use varying proportions of the two rubber compounds. There are some manufacturers who use hypalon as the only material for coating the base fabric and, with improved methods of gluing, this rubber is becoming the favoured type of inflatable boat fabric.

COLOUR CONSCIOUS

In the early days of inflatable boat manufacture black was the only viable colour for the neoprene rubber because it had a fair amount of carbon black added to it to get the necessary strength characteristics. Hypalon is much more flexible in terms of colour and although the preferred colour for the majority of modern boats is still a very practical grey, it is possible to get good quality rubbers in a wide variety of colours including whites and bright yellows. However red or orange probably remains the most popular colour after grey and this reflects the ability for this colour to stand out at sea and make the boat visible to other craft.

Inflation valves

Inflation valves come in a variety of forms, some manufacturers make their own whilst others buy in proprietary products. The main characteristics of all inflation valves are similar and they have three components.

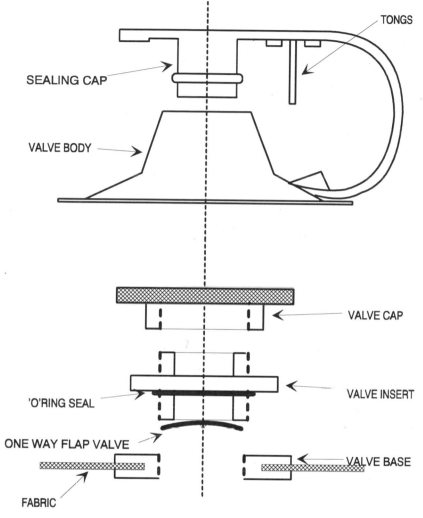

TONGS

SEALING CAP

VALVE BODY

VALVE CAP

VALVE INSERT

'O'RING SEAL

ONE WAY FLAP VALVE

VALVE BASE

FABRIC

Alternative types of inflation valve. The top valve is moulded from rubber whilst the lower type uses metal or plastic components.

First there is the insert which is glued or screwed into the fabric of the air tube. This usually comes in two parts, one inside and one outside and when the two are screwed up together a seal is formed around the rubber fabric. There is an inside screw thread in this insert and a landing flange. Into this aperture is screwed the main body of the valves which has a rubber diaphragm flap valve which deforms to let air in through the valve. The pressure inside forces this diaphragm against the valve body to seal the valve and prevent air leaking outwards. This valve itself makes an adequate seal during the pumping up operation but if left like this it would probably allow air to escape when the boat was pounding in a seaway. To make a positive seal a cap is fitted over the valve which is screwed down against a flexible washer. This cap is usually attached to the flange by means of a small cord or chain to prevent it getting lost when it is unscrewed for inflation. For deflating the boat, the whole valve body is removed and this lets the air escape freely.

Inflation valves are commonly made of plastic which resists corrosion and which can happily cope with the low pressures involved. Both stainless steel and brass have been used for inflation valves but the cost of these materials is rarely justified. Moulded rubber valves are also used and provide a material which is more compatible with the tube fabric. There are two principle types of valve which both operate on the same principle as described, but one stands proud from the tube and the other is virtually flush. There is a lot to be said for the flush type which maintains a virtual smooth continuity of the tube, but on the other hand, the protruding type of valve is easier to find and identify and is easier to use. When inflating the boat, the valve cap is simply unscrewed and the pipe from the inflation bellows is applied - usually a simple push fit into the valve aperture. The one way valve allows air to go in but prevents it escaping back into the bellows.

Some boats are fitted with a relief valve. This prevents over-inflation but is intended more for the purpose of relieving the air pressure inside the tube automatically if it should rise to unacceptably high levels if the boat is left out in a hot sun. The problem with these relief valves is that whilst they will happily let air out when the pressure rises they don't take air back in when the boat cools off; so when these valves are fitted you can find yourself constantly inflating the boat to restore the pressure when the boat has cooled. These days the improved construction fabrics can happily cope with much higher pressures and so relief valves tend to be used only on boats which have gas bottle inflation where they relieve any excess

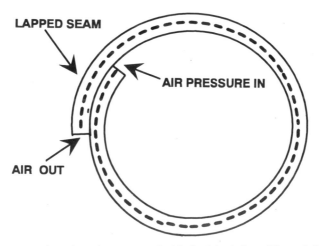

Wicking occurs when air under pressure inside the tube is forced through the reinforcing fabric and finds its way to the outside. Taping over the joints both inside and out is the way to prevent wicking.

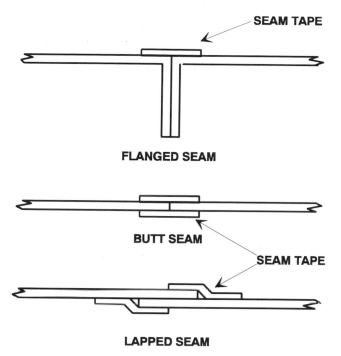

Alternative methods of creating seams in the tube fabric. The method most commonly used is the lapped seam.

pressure during inflation. The reduction in the use of black fabric, which attracts higher temperatures to the air tube because of its capacity to absorb heat, also helps in this situation. The absence of relief valves means that there are less things to go wrong.

Problem areas

Whilst the concept of the inflatable boat looks very simple there can be a number of problem areas in their design and construction. It is in the way that these problems are solved in the building of the boat which tends to denote the quality of the finished product and these are worth looking at in more detail.

Wicking is a tendency for air to travel through the reinforcing fabric lengthwise. During the calendaring process, minute air channels can be left within the base fabric and these can allow air to pass through, entering at one cut edge inside the tube and exiting at a cut edge outside the tube. On a well-made boat this problem is solved by taping the seam edges inside and outside with thin neoprene or hypalon tape. It adds to the work of building but it helps to maintain the airtight integrity of the tube. On the outside this tape also helps to prevent seam edges from lifting if they snag on a sharp edge and make a tidier finish to the boat.

The inflatable tubes used in the construction of the boat have to be built up as cylinders or cones. These are the only shape that can be made without getting wrinkles in the tube. Designers have become clever at developing the required boat-like shape of the finished product. However, problem areas occur when the angle of the tube has to change, perhaps in two planes where the tube bends inwards and upwards at the bow. Inevitably the fabric has to be coerced into the correct shape and skilful assembly can make this possible. One way to tell the difference between a well-made and a less well-made boat is to partially deflate it and see the wrinkles that form in the inflatable tubes. On a good boat they should be minimal and will be largely covered by the taping, but on a poorly-made boat they will be very evident. One reason why higher inflation pressures are often recommended by manufacturers is to iron out these wrinkles rather than for practical operational reasons.

Tube diameter is a compromise area in inflatable boat design. Obviously, a large diameter tube is going to give a better cushioning effect and provide higher sides and better protection to the boat. However, the larger diameter tube will also reduce the internal space within the boat. Tubes are normally between 15 and 20 in (38 and 50 cm) in diameter although they will obviously be less on smaller boats particularly those of the dinghy type.

Internal bladders are used on some inflatable boat designs, rather like the inner tube on a car tyre. There are two approaches to bladders, one is used to divide up the air chamber to improve the safety factor and reduce the need for internal bulkheads in the tubes. These bladders would tend to be made from the same material as the air tubes themselves as they can be exposed to the full pressure. The alternative is the inner tube approach where the bladder fills the full space in the tube and the tube itself does not have to be airtight. This was one approach on earlier boats to help compensate for poor quality fabric but it is difficult to get the bladder to deploy properly and it tends to add to the cost so it is rarely found these days.

Fixtures and fittings

The transom on inflatable boats is normally made from plywood, material which can quite happily take the stress of even powerful engines. The varnished wood transoms often seen on inflatables look attractive but can create maintenance problems and often the plywood is sheathed in GRP. The transom is simply glued in place via flanges at either side and it is a tribute to the modern adhesives used in inflatable boats that they remain firm under stress. A drain hole may be fitted low down in the transom so that when the boat is planing any water inside the boat can drain out. At slow speed, water will flow back in so a plug (usually of the screw type) is necessary to fill the hole. Various types of self-draining systems have been developed but whilst these are successful in removing water from inside the boat, they rarely completely seal the aperture to prevent water from coming in, and so are not completely successful. There are various systems such as flap valves and raspberry valves but these have to be held shut either by a spring or the material from which they are constructed and if they are designed to open under the very low pressure of water trying to drain out they don't create an effective seal to stop the water coming in. It is difficult to operate a screw-type drain when you are going along at sea at speed, and one of the better solutions is to have a 'trouser leg' or 'elephant's trunk' drain which is simply a tube of soft rubber fabric which is fitted outside around the hole cut in the transom. When in the closed position this is held up against the transom by a piece of line and simply by letting this line go the tube drops down and allows water to drain out. Like most things with inflatable boats, it is a simple solution like this which is often the most effective.

The ride of an inflatable boat is usually quite harsh even though the air tubes themselves do provide a degree of cushioning against the impact with waves. The hard wood or GRP floors can be very bruising in this situation and whilst some people use the tubes for seating, you are a bit vulnerable sitting on them when a boat is bouncing in a seaway and it is very hard to get a secure grip against being thrown overboard. You are much more secure sitting inside the boat and often a foam mattress is fitted over the floor to provide some cushioning against the hard surface of the floor. The foam in this mattress should be of the non-absorbent type (ie closed cell foam) so that it doesn't act like a sponge to soak up an enormous quantity of water and add to the weight of the boat. It should be secured in place fairly firmly perhaps with Velcro, in order to stop it moving and ending up in a heap at the back end of the boat. An inflatable mattress could be used but this tends to be very bouncy.

An alternative used in some sports inflatables is to fit seats and remote steering and throttle systems. The seats are often themselves inflatable and fitted towards the forward part of the boat. If they are to be effective, they need a secure back rest so that you have something against which to brace yourself against the movement of the boat. A good secure footrest is also very desirable so that you can brace your body between these two points, leaving your hands relatively free for the control of the boat. Firmer, rigid seats and even proper steering consoles are possibilities on larger inflatables, but it is not always easy to secure these items to the floorboards which have to be allowed to flex to a degree.

For sitting on the tubes handholds are essential and these are also useful for carrying the boat. There are two types of handhold generally used: rigid and flexible. Without doubt, the rigid type, usually made from moulded rubber, are the best because you can both push and pull against them and maintain a secure grip. The flexible type are fine when you want to pull but they can be very hard on the knuckles where these abrade against the tube material. You can never have too many handholds but they have to be restricted and you need to plan their location very carefully. Well placed handholds can make all the difference to your comfort in the boat. These handholds are normally strong enough to be used as mooring points when alongside but for anchoring and towing you need something stronger. A metal bow ring is usually glued on to the hull for this purpose but this should not be relied on completely and the rope should also be secured inboard.

In general, the concept of the inflatable is one of simplicity. The more complexity you put into the boat the more there is to go wrong. Tiller steering and hand-starting engines, which do not need batteries, make the inflatable boat a very effective and straightforward tool for operating in conditions and situations where more conventional boats might find it difficult. It is probably this concept of simplicity which is the reason why outboard motors are used on the vast majority of inflatables. There have been attempts to use small inboard engines boarded to the transom and even waterjet propulsion, and other concepts in inflatables but they have not really been successful. It is when you come to the rigid inflatable that many of these more advanced concepts can be used and this is what we will look at next.

CHAPTER 3

RIGID INFLATABLE BOAT (RIB) DESIGN AND DEVELOPMENT

Most of what has been said in the last chapter about air tube construction, materials and adhesives applies equally to the air tube of the rigid inflatable. Whilst the air tube is developed and constructed in the same way, there is however, a significant difference in the way the tube is used, because in the RIB the air tube is not a structural member. In the inflatable the air tube provides much of the longitudinal stiffness in the boat and therefore the pressure at which it operates is quite critical. In the rigid inflatable, the purpose of the air tube is to:

- Keep the water out
- Give continuity of the hull shape above the water line
- Provide the variable geometry shape
- Act as a fender.

The pressure in the air tube is not critical to any of these functions except perhaps the variable geometry. In most cases though, the air tube is very hard, usually between 3 and 4 psi. This might improve the appearance of the boat and help to smooth out any wrinkles in the fabric due to casual construction or poor design, but it does little to help the performance and, indeed, this high pressure can detract from performance in rough seas.

Tube pressures

Because the air tube is not required for structural purposes in the RIB, using a high air pressure means that the user can lose the benefit of the variable geometry factor found in these boats. Without doubt, the rigid inflatable is one of the most effective and seaworthy craft on the water today and much of this effectiveness comes from the ability of the air tube to absorb impact from both waves and when alongside other craft. If the boat is operated with lower air pressures in the inflatable tubes, around 1.5 to 2 psi, this will greatly increase this variable geometry effect by allowing the tubes to deform on impact. Lower air pressures also help when going alongside and help to reduce the bounce which can occur when the boat touches a jetty. With tubes inflated hard, the boat will bounce off as soon as it touches, often before you can get a line ashore. Softer air tubes will help to absorb the shock and reduce the bounce effect of the tubes. Tubes operated at a lower air pressure will also be less susceptible to puncturing if the boat hits a sharp object.

When driving in the open sea in waves, a lower air pressure, particularly in the forward compartments can be beneficial. The pressure should not be reduced to the point where the air tube becomes flabby and sags, but a good estimation of the correct pressure can be made when you knock the tube and you don't get the hard feeling of the drum-tight rebound found with an inflated tube at high pressure. At lower pressures, the water in the waves flowing up the rigid hull and over the lower surface of the air tube will be able to distort the tube and so find a smoother path. When the boat runs down the face of a following sea and hits the wave in front, the softer tube will provide a more gradual transition into the wave. In this situation there will be very little loss of buoyancy, and the boat should lift more smoothly to the next wave. Finally, there will be less bounciness in the ride as the air tubes on either side alternatively provide the stabilising effect which is an important characteristic of rigid inflatable performance.

The marriage of air tubes and rigid hull

In trying to understand why the rigid inflatable is such a good boat, there is another aspect of the relationship between the air tube and the rigid hull which is quite critical to performance. When the boat is at rest in its normal

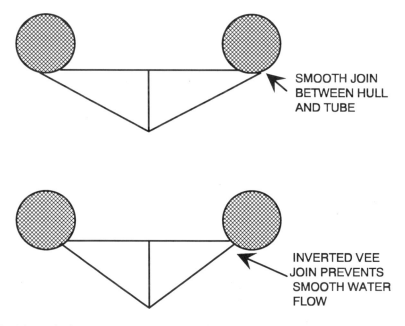

SMOOTH JOIN
BETWEEN HULL
AND TUBE

INVERTED VEE
JOIN PREVENTS
SMOOTH WATER
FLOW

When the tube at the bow creates a reverse turn in relation to the bottom of the hull, it can generate a great deal of spray when driven over-enthusiastically in a following sea. For best seakeeping, the tube and the hull should have a comfortable interface which allows water to flow smoothly over them.

loaded condition in calm water, then the air tubes at the stern of the boat should be just clear of the water. It is the rigid part of the hull which provides the effective planing surface, and if the air tubes are mounted too low then they will create increased and unnecessary drag as the boat is coming on to the plane without assisting very much in the way of increasing the effective planing area. When on the plane, the rigid deep vee hull will normally provide adequate stability because it is then dynamically supported, but the air tubes are always there to provide additional stability and a strong righting moment if the boat does heel over too far under the influence of waves.

Another important design consideration is the angle at which the rigid and inflatable surfaces meet where the tube is attached to the hull on the outside of the boat. On some designs, this meeting point creates a gull wing shape when looked at in transverse section, which may be fairly effective from a stability point of view, but does not give the water a smooth path when exiting from the hull. This type of design may provide more space on deck but it can lead to a harsher and more pounding ride. To a certain extent this pounding will be absorbed by the air tube flexing upwards. The same type of relationship between the inflatable tube and the rigid hull is also found at the bow on many designs and here a sudden change of section can be responsible for a harsher ride when operating in head or following seas. This rougher ride could be modified to a certain extent by lowering the air pressure in the tube so that it deforms and creates a smoother path for the water flow.

The alternative to the gull wing hull shape is to mount the air tubes higher

This Italian rigid inflatable demonstrates how the air tubes can be fully integrated into the hull and superstructure to give clean, smooth lines and internal cabin space.

and more inboard so that there is a close continuity in upward line of the deep vee hull which flows smoothly into the air tube shape and creates a streamlined and compatible path for the water flow exiting from the hull. The same sort of continuity of line can be achieved at the bow and there is no doubt that rigid inflatables which follow this sort of configuration will have a softer ride in open seas and will be more effective as sea-going boats. Against this has to be balanced the fact that because the air tube is mounted further inboard, the fendering provided by the air tube may be less effective and it is possible for the air tube to distort and allow the rigid part of the hull to come in contact with whatever the boat is going alongside. In any fendering situation the air tube does tend to 'roll' inboard, particularly when mounted in the higher position on the rigid section of the hull where there is less resistance to it rolling inboard. The designers have to find a compromise between these two extremes and, as a general rule, the extremity of the rigid hull should not extend outward beyond the centreline of the air tube.

A further factor which must be brought into this equation is the way in which the air tube is mounted on the hull. There is a variety of methods of attachment but the two basic systems are

1   The air tube is mounted into a curved channel moulded into the angle between the hull and the deck of the rigid hull.

2   An internal bulwark is provided on the rigid hull and the air tube is mounted external to this.

Both of these concepts have merit and in the first type the air tube has much more freedom to deform and thus can provide more effective variable geometry. This type of boat is also lighter but the air tube does tend to impinge more on the internal deck space of the boat. With the bulwark type of mounting the interior space on the deck is clearly defined and the bulwark can also provide a securing point for internal structures. With this type of installation, the air tube tends to adopt a more D-shaped cross section but invariably there is an uncomfortable angle between the bottom of the tube and the rigid hull and, amongst inflatable boat designers, this bulwark concept seems to be less attractive. The vast majority of modern rigid inflatables use the first of these two alternatives although one reason for this may be that it is cheaper.

Another advantage of the bulwark concept is that it does make mounting the tube much easier, and this is particularly the case if the air tube is mounted for easy removal and replacement. It is possible to use channels attached to the bulwark into which corresponding protrusions on the air tube can be inserted, starting at the bow and working aft. Another option is to have identical side tubes and a separate inflatable section at the bow. This means that tube replacement can be done on a piecemeal basis and by making the two side tubes identical they become interchangeable which can reduce the spares requirement. Such a design could be more attractive for a rigid inflatable carried aboard a mother ship where it is important to keep the RIB operational at all times. With such a system, tube damage can be repaired by replacement.

With the more conventional type of rigid inflatable where the air tube is in one piece and there is no internal bulwark fitted to the boat, then there are three alternative ways of attaching the tube. The first, and simplest, is to glue the tube in place along the landing surface moulded into the rigid part of the hull. Gusset strips are glued top and bottom to reduce the peeling strain on the glued surface. This is a very effective means of attachment which will stand the test of time, but it does make life difficult if the tube gets damaged to the point where it needs replacement. An alternative is to have a bolted flange top and bottom whereby an attachment strip on the air tube at the top and bottom of the joint is bolted under a stainless steel strip, with the bolts picking up on a metal strip, moulded into the fibreglass hull. This is a time consuming and relatively expensive system of attachment but it does enable the tube to be removed reasonably quickly and replaced. The third method is to use the channel slot system similar to that described with the bulwark boats. Alternatively, this channel system can be used in conjunction with a bolting system.

Most manufacturers have developed their own system which has stood the test of time; the main choice facing a buyer of rigid inflatables is whether the air tube should be permanently fixed in place or should be removable for replacement. Pleasure users will probably opt for the permanently fixed tube because this tends to be cheaper, whereas professional users may prefer the easily replaceable tube because their boats tend to suffer more abuse causing tube damage.

Foam-filled tubes

Another factor which has to be considered with rigid inflatables is whether to opt for the inflatable air tube or go for the foam-filled version, the latter concept often being derogatively termed 'bumper boats' by the purist RIB manufacturers. These foam-filled tubes do not have the ability to deform like the inflatable tube and the variable geometry aspect of the rigid inflatable is lost. The term 'bumper boat' derives from the fact that the foam-filled tubes act primarily as fenders. The bumper boat concept has been developed quite extensively by many boat designers and, in some designs, the foam tube is unashamedly added to the outside of the hull solely as a fender. At the other end of the scale there are designs which look exactly like rigid inflatables but use the foam tube which, though much less resilient than an air-filled tube, is less susceptible to damage and being put out of action. Obviously, the foam-filled tube can be damaged but it tends to retain its shape integrity in this condition, and the foam is a type which will not absorb water, so that the boat can remain operational. To a large degree, the bulwark type of rigid inflatable can also remain effective following damage to the air tube, but the same applies to the alternative type of RIB where the air tube is compartmentalised. Any damage to the tube only effects a relatively small part and the boat can

A cross-section of a foam filled tube. The outside skin provides the abrasion resistance. The characteristics of the tube can be varied by changing the density of the foam and the size of the internal void.

generally remain operational, although the ride may be much wetter, and the boat will have to be driven with more care.

In the bumper boat concept, the foam filled tube is usually built inside out. The tube is based on a tube of foam, usually PVC, which is slightly resilient. The air space left at the centre of the tube also helps to make the finished tube more resilient. Once the foam has been cut to shape and assembled it is sheathed, usually with a tough polyurethene coating. On some boats the 'tube' is constructed from moulded plastic sections. These sections are rather like fenders or mooring buoys and they have a small inflation valve for topping up the air pressure. Because these take the form of modular and interlocking units, the tube is built up from a series of sections which are strapped in place and which can be quickly replaced individually in the event of damage. Again, the resilience of this type of tube is not as good as the fully inflatable type and these alternative types of tube are more for professional use where there is a greater concern over tube damage and probably a greater risk. With careful driving, the risk of damage to the tube, however it is constructed is not high and the main priority in the design should be the performance of the boat rather than its ease of repair.

The rigid hull

The rigid part of the hull of a RIB is generally constructed in GRP these days although both wood and aluminium have been used in earlier designs. Aluminium is still used in some larger RIBs; it is best suited to

A rigid inflatable built with a bulwark inside the tube. The hull on this boat is constructed from aluminium and the 'tube' is made up from polyethelene moulded sections.

one-off designs and prototype construction. For general production boats, GRP is now widely used and it offers the possibility of moulding complex shapes at moderate cost. Strength is a very important factor in the construction of the rigid part of the hull because it is this structure which provides the rigid inflatable with its longitudinal strength. Because rigid inflatables tend to be driven much harder than conventional boats, this longitudinal strength is very critical. Compared with conventional boats, however, the cross section of the hull is much smaller, and so it is much harder to get adequate strength within the limits of a very shallow hull depth. Deep longitudinal stringers inside the hull provide most of this strength. Whilst the deck contributes to the strength of the structure, because it is moulded as a separate unit and attached afterwards, it is not always easy to attach the deck in a way in which the deck and hull can form a fully integrated structural unit. Access also has to be provided in the deck for fitting fuel tanks, and the engine or engines where these are mounted inboard. Smaller rigid inflatables, powered by outboards, often have nothing installed inside the hull itself, so it is possible to make a more integrated structure.

Some rigid inflatables, notably the Avon Seariders, use part of the space inside the rigid part of the hull as a ballast tank. This space is filled and emptied automatically through a large flooding hole in the transom. It fills when the boat is at rest and drains as the boat comes on to the plane. In this way, the ballast can automatically increase the stability and lower the freeboard at rest; the lowered freeboard making it easier to climb back on

The internal construction of a rigid inflatable hull showing the deep frames and stringers and the fuel tanks installed under the deck.

board after a swim or dive or to recover casualties. The system works well in practice but boats of this type should not be left lying afloat because weed and barnacles will grow inside the ballast space and they can be very difficult to remove. The ballast tank also prevents fuel tanks from being stowed under the deck.

Most rigid inflatable hulls are constructed from glass fibre using polyester resins but for high performance or where light weight is particularly significant, then Kevlar and carbon fibres are used for critical areas of the hull; epoxy resins will often be used to give a higher strength laminate. The transom is almost invariably constructed from plywood faced on either side with laminate; plywood being a suitable material to allow through bolting for the engine mounts without the laminate compressing. For the longitudinal stringers and transverse stiffening frames, foam filled laminate structures may be used, but plywood can be used as an alternative although it is considerably heavier. Void spaces within the rigid part of the hull are often filled with foam which helps to maintain buoyancy if the hull should get damaged. However it is important to use the right type of foam; very rigid foam should be avoided because it tends to break up under the slight flexing which is always apparent in a hull when operating in a seaway. The foam should be at least slightly resilient and should be of the closed cell type so that it doesn't absorb water. Where foam is not used then the hull is often divided into a number of watertight compartments so that any damage will remain local and the main structure and integrity of the boat will remain.

Deep-vee hulls are almost invariably used on rigid inflatables. Some of the smaller types around 3 or 4 metres in length may have only a mod-

A cutaway of a rigid inflatable hull showing the vertical stringers in the rigid section of the hull and the baffle in the air tube.

erate vee, perhaps with a 12 or 15° deadrise, but for boats designed for serious use at sea then a deadrise between 20 and 25° is more normal. This deep vee helps to cushion the impact with waves, but against this has to be balanced the fact that the deeper the vee, the less efficient the planing surface. With modern lightweight engines, it is not difficult to install adequate power to give the required performance whilst still retaining the cushioning effect of the deep-vee.

There are many variations on the deep vee hull which different manufacturers use. One which was used on the original RIB, the Atlantic 21, had a flattened area at the apex of the vee. This helped to reduce the draft of the hull and make it more suitable for beach launching. Such a flattened surface also helps to give more efficient planing, but the water flow round such a hull shape tends to be more turbulent. For a single-engine rigid inflatable, such a flattened surface may be viable because it means an outboard engine can be mounted slightly higher; with twin screw outboard boats, the conventional deep vee is the preferred shape.

Spray rails are an essential part of any deep-vee hull and these are positioned to help peel the water away from the hull surface. They are located mainly in the forward part of the hull and help generate lift as it rises from the water; this in turn helps to reduce the wetted surface area of the hull and hence reduce the friction resistance and give improved performance. Spray rails can also help to reduce the spray emanating from the hull forward, but the joint between the rigid hull and the air tube also helps keep the spray under control. They also help to stabilise the deep vee hull transversely. The hull shape itself encourages this stability because if the boat heels over, the hull on that side has a lower deadrise and so generates

The ultimate test for a rigid inflatable – operating without the inflatable tube! It is the rigid section of the hull which creates the planing surface and the tubes should be clear of the water. *Photo: Carson.*

more lift to create a righting moment. Spray rails encourage this by creating an inverted vee shape where the bottom of the rail meets the hull which generates good lift.

We have already looked at the meeting point between the rigid hull and the air tube and the angle which is formed here, but some boatbuilders introduce additional chines or steps in the rigid section of the hull either just below the attachment point, or at that point, in order to produce a better transitional shape between the two components of the hull.

At the bow the hull shape should be reasonably full. Here a balance has to be struck between the fine shape, which cuts through the waves without generating too much lift when going into a head sea, and the fuller shape required for operating in a following sea. In general, because of the relatively short hulls involved, rigid inflatable designers tend to go for a fuller hull shape, working on the basis that it is better for the hull to fly off a wave than to bury itself at the bow. The air tube provides a good reserve of buoyancy in all situations and this is one aspect of the design which makes the RIB so adaptable and suitable for differing conditions. Some designers may exploit this forgiving aspect of rigid inflatables, making them less than careful about the hull shapes they are developing.

The most important factor in rigid inflatable design is the relationship between the rigid section and the inflatable section, and looking at some rigid inflatable designs it would appear that this relationship is developed by accident rather than design. The sheer line, which is the angle or curve of the deck when seen from the side can be another important aspect of design. The simple solution here is to have a straight sheer line which means that the tube can also be a straight line which is cheaper and simpler to construct. However if a straight sheer is used, this can compromise the hull shape and tends to leave a lower bow than may be ideal for operating in waves. A slight curve in the sheer line can be accommodated by a straight tube but to get the best sheer line the tube has to be constructed with both an upward and an incurving angle towards the bow.

Inboard or outboard engines?

Compared with a pure inflatable, the rigid hull incorporated into the design makes it much easier to accommodate a variety of machinery concepts into the rigid inflatable and these span the whole range of possibilities available on the market today. Whilst the outboard motor is still the most popular type of engine used on RIBs and is the one used almost without exception on smaller rigid inflatables, the diesel engine is growing in popularity, particularly amongst professional users. The outboard motor may have benefits in terms of initial costs but it also incurs expensive fuel costs. For the professional user, the diesel engine is favoured because it uses a compatible fuel with the mother ship it is often carried on. The diesel fuel is also much safer to carry on board a mother ship than petrol and, perhaps equally important, the engineers on board the ship are more familiar with diesel engines than they are with the very sensitive engineering found on outboard motors.

On most RIBs of 6 metres or over it is possible to fit twin outboards and this offers a measure of safety and reduces the impact of any engine failure. With diesel engines, the additional weight and size of the machinery tends to mean that only a single engine can be installed except on the largest of rigid inflatables. However modern diesel engines are getting smaller and lighter all the time. They have improved power to weight ratios so that it is now becoming practical to fit twin diesel engines on rigid inflatables of 7 or 8 metres in length which probably gives the ultimate in engine reliability and safety. In terms of propulsion, both stern drive legs and water jets are used in conjunction with these diesel engines.

With the increasing variety of machinery available for rigid inflatables, the designer's job can become more difficult when he is expected to adapt a standard design to accommodate the various options. The main choice is between inboard and outboard engines and with inboard engines an engine housing has to be incorporated into the deck area because the engine rises above the deck level. Air intakes also have to be incorporated because engines won't run without an air supply, but we will look at the details of the machinery installation later on. Suffice to say that the installation of an inboard engine or engines can have a significant impact on the way the deck of the boat is laid out.

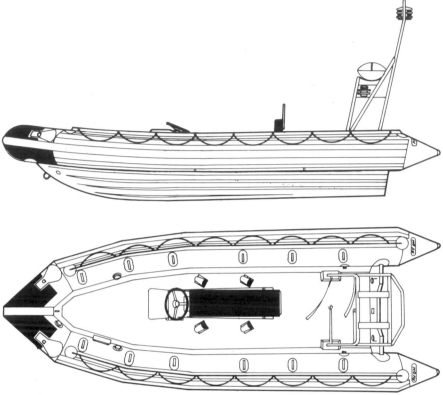

An Avon RIB designed as a rescue boat for offshore oil operations. Note the layout of the footholds, the slightly offset steering console and seats (to counteract the propeller torque) and the self-righting equipment.

Saddle seating

It was saddle seating which made one of the major contributions towards RIB design and this type of seating is incorporated into most rigid inflatables today. Saddle seating can range from the simple concept of a one-man or two-man seat with a very basic steering console designed into the forward end of it. This is the type of seating used on smaller RIBs, whereas larger models which may have to accommodate a larger crew may use a Y or delta-shaped saddle seat with the helmsman at the forward end on his own and two crew members side by side on the arms of the Y. If more crew members have to be accommodated, then further seats on the arms of the Y can be added. The essential criteria for any seating in a rigid inflatable is that the crew should be as well provided for as the helmsman. With the saddle seat adequately padded with non-springing foam, a crew member is well secured against the motion of the boat. The saddle seat itself can be gripped with the knees but toe straps which are simple loops fastened to the deck, provide a good additional grip. A handhold bar is usually fitted across the seat in front of the crew member and should be of rigid material so that he can push or pull against it to steady himself. Backrests are also incorporated into some seat designs which can help the crew man to brace himself more securely.

With this type of layout, a crew member can have at least one hand free to perform other duties such as using a radio or navigation equipment, and it is possible to be comfortable for two or three hours at a time with this type of seating. The driver's position is equally critical and again, with the saddle seat and the toe straps, he can steady himself well against the motion of the boat leaving both hands free for the vital control of the boat. The steering wheel is quite straightforward in terms of operation but it needs to be positioned and angled carefully for optimum comfort. An angle of 30 – 40° from the horizontal is best. The throttle location is much more critical as using the throttle correctly is an essential element in driving a rigid inflatable. Normally, a single lever throttle is used which controls both throttle and gears. When positioning the throttle, it is the 'ahead' position which is used most of the time at sea, and this should be placed where it is easiest to use. It can be very tiring constantly holding your arm up to use the throttle and, ideally, some sort of arm support in the vicinity of the throttle can be a great help both to help steady the arm against the motion of the boat but also to provide a rest so that the constant use of the throttle can be maintained over long periods.

Protection from the weather

The type of saddle seating found on most small RIBs leaves the crew very exposed to the elements, which can be quite acceptable in warmer conditions but in colder weather this exposure can rapidly reduce the effectiveness of the crew. A windscreen can be fitted on a console forward of the saddle seating, but it has to be fairly high and wide to be effective. Looking through a windscreen can reduce the clear vision which is essential for reading sea conditions and driving the RIB effectively. An alternative, found on some leisure-orientated rigid inflatables, is to use a two-man console fitted with a screen, with the crew sitting or standing side by side. A standing driving position can be quite effective on a RIB, although there is a tendency for the helmsman to use the steering wheel as a hand hold and the other hand may not be as free as it ought to be for using the throttles. In the design of a windscreen or other crew protection it is important to remember that spray rarely comes directly over the bow but is much more likely from an angle on the bow as the wind catches the spray and blows it back on board.

A further alternative is to fit a wheelhouse, or at least a wheelhouse shelter to give the crew protection, and this is now a feasible proposition on rigid inflatables as small as 8 metres in length. Using a wheelhouse takes the RIB into a whole new area as far as its potential and use is concerned; it means that the crew can operate effectively for considerably longer periods because they are in a more protected environment. The steering console and saddle seat can be fitted under cover inside the wheelhouse. Windscreen wipers will be an important feature of any wheelhouse design to give good visibility and it is equally important that the windows should be very wide with the roof supports being as narrow as possible to avoid blind spots in the helmsman's vision. Because the crew are surrounded by a variety of hard surfaces in a wheelhouse, it is important that any edges are well padded to prevent injuries if the crew get thrown about; also sound damping is important if the crew are to operate for long periods satisfactorily. As always, with any design of control and seating arrangements it is the small details which are very important to the comfort and safety of the crew. If you create the right environment for a helmsman to operate effectively and safely then the performance from the rigid inflatable will be improved accordingly.

The deck and its fittings

The deck of the rigid inflatable is normally self draining because the deck level is above the outside water level. If a full width transom is fitted, then provision must be made for water to drain out rapidly and effectively either through or over the transom. Stowage for equipment can usually be catered for either inside or under the console or seating, but an alternative is to fit a locker into the vee at the bow; this can be useful for anchor and line stowage. A good strong mooring post forward is a useful feature to provide a secure attachment for mooring or anchoring; it is also important if the boat has to be towed. Such a mooring post is also vital if the rigid inflatable is launched from a mother ship because this will be the main attachment for the painter. In this situation there should be room for the crew member handling this painter to position himself so that he can handle the painter effectively and quickly. Otherwise the deck area forward is usually left clear, although there may attachment points for securing cargo and/or passengers and survivors, depending on the use of the boat. Aft there is often a roll bar or a frame fitted which serves a variety of functions. This is usually constructed from tubular aluminium or stainless steel and is bolted down to the deck or the transom. It provides a mounting point for navigation lights, and radio and navigation equipment antennae. Capsize righting equipment can be mounted on the roll bar and it can also act as the securing point for mooring lines aft and even an attachment for a towing post.

The rigid part of a RIB makes it much easier to make strong attachments for deck fittings and equipment; this is an area where the rigid inflatable has the edge over the pure inflatable. The introduction of the rigid hull means that this type of craft is an excellent compromise between the inflatable and the rigid hull boat and some designs are now moving closer to the more conventional craft by adding a GRP moulded structure above and inside the air tube and integrating with it. In the bow area this can create a cabin and it may extend over the bow and link up with the rigid hull to form a solid bow. The options within the rigid inflatable concept seem to be endless. Whilst it was originally conceived as a compromise, the RIB has now moved way beyond that point to where it is a boat concept on its own; it now not only matches the performance of the types of boat from which it was developed, but in most cases far exceeds it. The rigid inflatable lends itself to performing in extreme conditions, and this needs to be taken into account when fitting out and installing equipment. It can be subjected to stresses far beyond those found in conventional craft and, if the outfitting is to be compatible with the performance, then nothing far short of the best quality materials and equipment must be used.

CHAPTER 4

ENGINES AND PROPULSION SYSTEMS

Lose propulsion in an inflatable or a RIB and, to a certain extent, you have lost the boat. The boat may not sink but you are in a very vulnerable position when you take into account the high rate of drift and the risk of capsize of these small boats. You face the same problems in a small inflatable dinghy when you can't make headway under oars. Without the propulsion you might as well be in a liferaft and your salvation tends to be in other people's hands rather than in your own. With this in mind, a reliable propulsion system on an inflatable or rigid inflatable is absolutely essential, which is why we will go through all the critical aspects of the installation in some detail. It is not too difficult to get things right and it needn't cost a lot of money but the important thing is not to leave anything to chance if you want to keep the machinery running.

Outboards

Outboard motors represent the main type of propulsion system in the inflatable and RIB market. As far as inflatables are concerned, outboards dominate the market almost completely, and this applies from the smallest to the largest inflatable boat. The vast majority of inflatables use a single engine installation but in the RIB sector there is a much wider choice of propulsion systems from single or twin outboards to single or twin inboard diesels, coupled to water jets or stern drives. There is a lot of merit in the outboard motor because it is a completely self-contained unit combining both engine and propulsion, and in the very small sizes, also incorporating the fuel tank. This means that the whole installation is a tried and tested unit, one where all the components are compatible and have been designed to operate together. The modern outboard is a far cry from some of the earlier versions where reliability was suspect; provided that you have installed the engine correctly and supply it with clean fuel, oil, and electrical power when necessary and keep it reasonably dry and serviced, then there is no reason why it shouldn't keep running reliably and smoothly.

From this you will gather that the outboard motor itself and its built-in propulsion system are inherently reliable. They are remarkably water resistant and in most cases you can play a hose over the engine even with

This inflatable dinghy has a small petrol outboard mounted on a bracket fitted over the stern tube. An ideal craft for inshore fine-weather fishing, provided the hook doesn't puncture the tube! *Photo: Avon.*

the hood off, and it will keep running, provided you don't stick the hose up the carburetor intake! This is a measure of how the outboard has developed in recent years, so you can assume that if it does stop for any reason, then the first thing to suspect is the external connections rather than the engine itself. Having said this, the outboard motors on inflatable boats and to a lesser extent on RIBs come in for considerably physical abuse. The motion of the boat can be very violent and, as far as inflatables are concerned, the fact that the outboard is mounted on a structure which is flexing adds to this physical punishment. In particular, its mounting brackets and fastenings can be vulnerable, so as the driver of an inflatable, try to give the outboard as easy a ride as possible. It can suffer particular strain when you fly the boat a long way out of the water or when you run up a beach or otherwise operate in shallow water where the outboard lower unit may ground at high speed. Here the vulnerable components are the mounting brackets and the securing bolts.

ENGINE MOUNTINGS

Smaller outboards up to 20 or 30 hp are simply clamped on to the transom or mounting bracket with clamping screws. A metal plate is fixed to the transom to spread the load of the clamping screws as they are screwed up tight; often the mounting bracket will have little serrated edges, where it butts against the transom on its rear side, which bite into the timber. These help to prevent sideways and up and down movement of the engine on the transom. Even on the smallest outboard it is important that you check the tightness of the clamps, certainly every time before you use the boat, and then perhaps every half an hour or so when you are at sea. These clamps will only be satisfactory when they are fully tight and any slight play which is allowed between the mounting brackets and the transom will start to magnify itself until the whole engine can become loose. To guard against the possibility of the engine leaping right off the boat, it is normal practice to have a securing chain between the engine bracket and the transom which will at least prevent you losing the engine altogether.

On larger outboard motors, the engine is not designed for quick and easy removal, partly because it is too heavy to carry around easily, but equally importantly because it needs to be bolted rather than clamped on to the transom. The forces involved with a larger outboard are too much for a clamping system to cope with adequately; clamps are rarely fitted on engines over 60 hp. Instead, there are brackets to locate the engine at the top of the transom to ensure that it is at the right height and then there are usually four or six stainless steel bolts through the transom to fix the engine securely in place. These bolts should be backed up by large washers inside the boat to spread the load and the transom will be stiffened in this area to help spread the stress and strain. The securing bolts should be fitted with lock washers, or locking nuts. On rigid inflatables, where it is often not practical or easy to get inside the hull to gain access to the inboard end of these bolts, the bolt head may be secured in place so that it cannot turn, and the nuts placed on the outside of the transom so that the engine can be easily removed. Every so often, these mounting bolts should be checked for tightness and to ensure that the lock nuts are adequately secured.

FUEL TANKS

Small outboard engines of up to 5 hp will often have an integral fuel tank which means that the fuel system has been tried and tested and will be reliable. With such a system, the only problems likely to develop may be dirt in the fuel and minor leaks in the fuel piping which should be checked for integrity every now and again. It is not easy to ensure that the fuel is clean at all times, but there is a fuel filter in the system which is usually mounted on the engine itself at a point close to the fuel pump. Where a gravity fuel feed is used, the filter will be close to the carburetor and these filters should be cleaned out at regular intervals. Any excessive amount of dirt which collects in the filter should be regarded with suspicion and could indicate that the fuel tank needs cleaning out.

With larger outboards, an external fuel supply is required and the options here are portable metal tanks of the type supplied by outboard motor manufacturers, flexible tanks made from special rubber, plastic or built-in tanks which may be constructed from aluminium or stainless steel. Rigid plastic tanks are now growing in popularity as they are cheaper and easy to carry or stow but they must comply with BS10-13 in UK and their use may be restricted in other countries. The manufacturers' metal tanks

Alternative types of fuel tank in an inflatable. The flexible tank (right) is much lighter and easier to stow than the steel tank. It also has no sharp edges but it is also considerably more expensive.

seem to work perfectly adequately in inflatables and cope with the rough ride, but the biggest problem with these tanks is securing them in place. They are best located at the aft end where the ride conditions are usually kinder, but here they can often present sharp edges on which the crew can hurt themselves and it can be quite difficult to tie them down adequately to the floor boards.

Elastic straps can rarely be secured tight enough to prevent the tanks moving under the motion of the boat and it is better to use webbing straps with a ratchet tightener. Secure the tanks really tightly because only a slight amount of play will get the tanks moving. There should be a piece of plywood or rubber matting under the tank to prevent wear and tear on the floor boards. The advantage of these tanks is that they can be taken ashore for refuelling and they have a fuel gauge built in so you know how much is left in the tank. The disadvantages of metal tanks are the sharp edges in the handles, the fact that they are usually made from mild steel which means that they will corrode in a salt atmosphere, and the difficulty of securing them adequately. On an inflatable they have to be stowed somewhere on the floor because this is the only area to which they can be secured. In a RIB there is much more scope for stowage and the saddle seating is often designed and dimensioned to accommodate these tanks where they are out of the way and yet readily accessible.

Flexible fuel tanks are a good idea but they are expensive. The special rubber, which has to be petrol-impervious, is costly and the tanks have to be made of quite thick rubber to stand up to the surge and physical stresses involved. These flexible fuel tanks come in a variety of shapes, some rather like a carrier bag with a built in handle, others long and tubular so that they can be secured along the inflatable tubes. They have no sharp edges apart from perhaps the filler cap, and there is no need for an air vent to allow air in to replace the fuel which is taken out. These air vents, necessary in rigid tanks, can be a source of water getting into the fuel under extreme conditions, but with the flexible tank, it simply collapses as it empties and no air need be taken in to replace the used fuel. A flexible tank still needs to be secured to give it a reasonable chance of survival and you have to watch carefully for chafe against any of the rigid members of the boat.

Built-in metal tanks are one of the best solutions but are really only practical as far as RIBs are concerned because there is no suitable space in an inflatable boat to install permanent tanks. The only exception might be if there is console seating fitted where tanks could be installed underneath. In rigid inflatables the permanent tanks could be mounted underneath the console or seating if they are required above decks, but normally they are installed inside the hull, securely attached to structural members and often supported by injected foam. Stainless steel is the preferred material for these tanks because of its resistance to corrosion and its better fatigue resistance compared with aluminium. Some form of external fuel gauge is necessary on these tanks and a breather pipe also has to be fitted to allow air to enter as the fuel is taken out, or for air to escape as the tank is filled. With a petrol tank, the breather pipe should be fitted with fine gauze at the outboard end; this helps to reduce any fire risk from fumes which could emanate from the pipe and also helps to prevent water entering the pipe and flowing into the tank.

FUEL LINES, PUMPS AND FILTERS

With outboard engines there is a need for a flexible pipe between the tank and the motor itself. On inflatable boats, the complete pipe will normally be flexible and this is one of the more vulnerable components in the boat. Unless it is routed carefully, it will have a nasty habit of getting trapped between the floor boards and the transom or crew members can sit or stand on it with the result that it can get damaged and leak petrol into the bottom of the boat, so it pays you to protect this fuel pipe very carefully.

The end fastenings on outboard fuel pipes are usually a push fitting which has an automatic seal comprising a spring-loaded ball valve, pressing on to a rubber O ring. This O ring serves to seal the ball valve when the pipe is disconnected and also makes a seal when the pipe is connected. A leak through this O ring when the pipe is disconnected may not be particularly serious but any leakage when the pipe is connected immediately allows air rather than fuel to be sucked into the engine and it will stop rapidly or, much more likely, it won't start in the first place. These O rings need careful inspection for damage at regular intervals and if you suspect that the engine is not getting adequate fuel or starts to misfire, then the O ring could be suspect, although running out of fuel would produce the same symptoms.

The fuel line is normally fitted with a priming bulb which is like a small manual pump which sucks fuel from the tank and feeds it to the carburetor. This priming is necessary before starting the engine, and once it starts, the engine-mounted fuel pump takes over the suction process. You can quickly feel when the priming process is complete because the rubber bulb tends to feel much firmer, but if you keep pumping and the bulb never seems to become hard, then immediately suspect that the O ring is damaged or that there is possibly dirt in the fuel which is preventing the little non-return valve in the priming bulb from sealing properly.

From the fuel line the fuel is routed first into a fuel filter and then into the carburetor. With a fixed installation on a rigid inflatable, there may be a fuel filter mounted external to the engine which both serves to trap any dirt in the fuel and also to separate any water which might be in the fuel. This same type of filter is sometimes found mounted on the transom of inflatable boats and the glass bulb of these filters provides a ready check for any contamination in the fuel. The engine-mounted fuel filter may also have a glass bulb so that it can be quickly checked for contamination, but you have to take off the engine hood to carry out the check. The engine fuel filters usually need to be dismantled with a spanner and it can be a tricky exercise to clean them at sea because you are usually hanging over the back of the boat and you only have to drop one of the components to render that engine completely immobile. Past this fuel filter there is little you can do about faults in the fuel system, but as it is a completely tried and tested unit, the chances of problems occurring beyond the fuel filter are relatively small.

POWER SUPPLIES AND WIRING

For small outboard motors up to about 50 hp you have a choice of manual or electric starting. Manual starting is the preferred system for smaller inflatables because it removes the need to carry a battery and the engine is full self-contained apart from the fuel tank. Batteries and inflatables are not particularly compatible; having to find suitable stowage for a battery can be even more difficult than trying to secure the fuel tanks. The very damp atmosphere or perhaps we should say, the wet atmosphere in an inflatable boat, is not conducive to the survival of electrical systems, and so if you want good engine reliability, there is a lot to be said for sticking to manual starting and not having any electrical system outside the engine itself.

If you need higher engine power than is available with manual starting engines, then it is worth considering a twin-engine installation rather than going up in size where electric starting is essential. You would need to consider this carefully because with a twin-engine installation you will probably need wheel steering. Whilst it is possible to engineer tiller steering and throttle control with a twin engine installation, this is not readily available as a standard unit and would normally have to be built to order. Also you will incur double costs when professional servicing is required. Whichever route you take when higher powered engines are required, it will add complication to the installation and means there is more to go wrong.

An unusual airport emergency unit, this Mersey River Rescue craft acts as a crash tender for Speke Airport which is sited right on the River Mersey. Even well loaded with liferafts for survivors, the powerful V8 5.8 litre sterndrive engine is capable of 38–40 knots. *Photo: Chinook.*

For many inflatables, a 50 hp engine provides more than adequate power and so you can stick with manual starting. For RIBs, installing a battery is much less of a problem and here twin manually-started outboards can offer a viable alternative because wheel steering and remote throttles are normally fitted to a rigid inflatable anyway. There can be other reasons for having a battery installed in an inflatable or a RIB, and if you want to operate at night, it could be essential for supplying power to navigation lights. Also, if you need a radio on board or electronic navigation equipment, then some form of power supply is essential.

If your power requirements are quite small, then you could manage with a battery which has been charged on shore and which has no connection with the engine. This certainly simplifies the installation and leaves you in the happy position of having a non-electric start engine, but it does mean charging the battery every time you go ashore and re-installing it. The biggest problem you face in either situation is to find a good stowage for the battery; in an inflatable, the only logical place is to fit it to the floorboards, preferably in a plastic box with a lid which gives the battery some protection from sea water. If you do install a battery in a box, then remember that the battery itself must be firmly secured to the floorboards to prevent movement in any direction. Just putting it in a box which is attached to the floor boards is inadequate because the battery will rattle around inside and eventually the wires will come loose, chafe, or break. When stowing a battery in a rigid inflatable you need the same careful approach and the battery must be securely clamped or bolted down to a rigid surface so that there cannot be any movement. Tying it down with a webbing strap is rarely adequate and certainly elastic cords are unsuitable; the best method is a properly bolted clamp system.

The wiring in these boats also presents problems, particularly the wiring that goes to and from an outboard because it has to be very flexible to accommodate the steering and tilting movement of the engine and at the same time it is very exposed. In particular, the heavy duty starter cables have to be of a special flexible type. The normal heavy duty semi-rigid starter motor wires found on other engines are definitely not suitable. The wiring must be protected from chafing against any sharp edges; one of the better approaches is to put the wiring inside a rubber tube.

All connections in the electrical system of an inflatable or RIB should be fully watertight otherwise corrosion and short circuiting will occur and you will have an unreliable system. This means fitting expensive and high quality components but anything less is a false economy. The only area in which you may not be able to achieve full watertightness is on the battery terminals but they should be well greased and protected with rubber or plastic boots. Electricity and water do not mix; the water always wins, so bear this in mind when installing or checking electrical systems on your boat.

ENGINE COOLING

The cooling water system is built into the engine so the main thing which you have to know is that it incorporates a pump in the lower part of the drive housing which uses a synthetic rubber impeller. Rubber impellers are not intended to be run dry and so, while you can briefly fire up the engine on dry land to make sure it is going to work, it must be cut immediately, otherwise the impeller gets hot and melts. The pump itself is cooled and lubricated by the water which it pumps through the engine. So if you need to run the engine on land, attach a hose to the connection designed to flush fresh water through the system.

One cooling system problem is blockage of the relatively fine grid of the water intake. Plastic bags are a notorious hazard in this respect. They wrap themselves around the front of the outboard drive leg, effectively blocking off the water supply. There is not a lot you can do about this except to keep your eyes peeled for debris when you are driving the boat and try to avoid areas where debris may be a hazard. Clearing debris from around the outboard is not particularly difficult. You simply tilt the engine up, clear the debris, put the outboard back down into the driving position and away you go. The main problem is in detecting the obstruction to the cooling water system before it does serious damage to the engine. With electric start engines, there is a warning light or alarm to indicate that the engine temperature is rising, but with manual outboards you don't have this luxury. You may not be aware of a problem until the engine starts to falter or stop. By this time there could be serious damage inside the engine because the precision machinery is very sensitive to changes in its operating environment. The only solution is to be sensitive to the performance of the engine and take note of any unexpected changes in engine sound or speed. Also, check the water outlet which is visible from the rear of the engine at regular intervals. The problem is less likely to be detected when you have remote steering and throttles, because then you are further away from the engines, but with this type of installation it is much more likely that you will have electric start engines with a warning light anyway.

Salt water is highly corrosive so it is advisable to flush the engine through with fresh water after each trip. Special fittings are available to either clamp around or fit over the water intake. You can then attach a hose to a nozzle on the outboard and run the water and engine simultaneously. Not only does this flush out the salt water in the cooling system, but it also allows you to run the engine on dry land where it is much easier to tune and make adjustments if this becomes necessary. If you adopt this procedure every time you come ashore, you will help to prolong the life of the engine. At the same time, take off the hood and check the exterior of the engine; dry it off and spray with silicone grease which will help to reduce the onset of corrosion, particularly around the fittings of the electrical system.

Outboards come in two sizes in terms of shaft length: long shaft and short shaft. Most inflatables will accept the short shaft engine and the transom height is built accordingly whereas RIBs tend to need the long shaft engine because of the deep vee hull. The transoms of all boats are designed to accept one or other of these engines. If you wish to fit twin engines, which are further out from the centreline, on a boat designed for a single engine, adjustment in the height of the engines may be necessary. If you are looking for the ultimate in performance there can be merit in raising the engines higher and allowing the propellers to operate in the surface piercing mode. Whilst you may gain something in terms of top end performance with this approach, you will find it harder to get the boat on to the plane and less responsive in rough seas.

DIESEL OUTBOARDS
The vast majority of outboards on the market today are two-stroke units which combine lightweight with high power. Four-stroke outboards are available in powers up to around 40 hp and these can provide a viable alternative with smoother and quieter running. They also offer considerably better fuel consumption than the two-stroke. Another option for powering inflatables and RIBs is the latest generation of diesel outboards. The diesel outboard is considerably heavier than its two stroke petrol counterpart, and for an inflatable boat, there is little incentive to change to a diesel outboard unless you use the boat a great deal, when the improved fuel economy could prove attractive. The initial cost of a diesel is around 50% more than a petrol outboard. Modern high-revving diesel engines have acceleration which can be almost as good as petrol outboards, and there is generally very good torque at lower speeds which helps to get the boat on to the plane. However, the throttle response is slower which could be an important factor when operating the boat in waves.

The diesel outboard benefits from improved reliability because there is no electrical system required to keep the engine running, but hand-starting a 40 hp diesel certainly requires more pull that starting the equivalent petrol engine. For rigid inflatables, the fuel economy may make it desirable to switch to a diesel outboard, also the compatibility and availability

The world's fastest rigid inflatable built in Italy by FB Design and Novamarine. This 47 footer is powered by twin Seatek diesels to give speeds in excess of 100 mph.

of the fuel could be a significant factor, particularly for commercial users or when the boat is operated from a mother ship. The use of diesel outboards tends to be restricted to smaller RIBs simply because of the limited power output available, but they certainly have their merits, particularly as an auxiliary source of power for a single-engined diesel inboard RIB.

Diesel inboard engines

The diesel inboard is used primarily by professionals because of its inherent reliability, its fuel economy and the compatibility of the fuel. Diesel inboard power is limited to rigid inflatables and is a comparatively new innovation because engines with a suitably high power to weight ratio are a recent development. Some of the early diesel powered RIBs would barely get on to the plane and had a top speed of probably no more than 25 knots, which as we shall see in the chapter on handling, is barely adequate for many sea conditions. As engine and boat performance always decrease with the passage of time, so the speed potential of these early diesel boats would drop below acceptable limits. Modern diesels can have a power to weight ratio of 2 kg:1 hp or less and this makes the diesel a very viable proposition. A growing market for diesel powered RIBs in the professional areas will inevitably spread down to the leisure market, although these diesel powered rigid inflatables are considerably more expensive than their outboard powered counterparts.

ENGINE MOUNTINGS

The stresses on a diesel engine in a RIB can be very high and particular care has to be taken over the engine mounts. Although it is possible to get reduced vibration and noise levels with flexible engine mounts, they can be stretched to their operating limits with some of the violent motions of a RIB and solid mounting is advisable but not essential. Fixed engine mounts obviate the need for flexible connections to the engine in terms of fuel and electrical supply, cooling water and exhaust. Whilst flexible sections will still be introduced into these systems, stress on the components will be less because the requirement for movement is minimal.

FUEL AND ELECTRICAL SYSTEMS

The fuel system will be very similar in many respects to that of an outboard engine using built-in tanks. There will certainly be a separate fuel filter in the line, and there could be two alternative tanks from which fuel can be drawn, which is helpful in a situation where there is contamination or damage to one tank. Greater precautions need to be taken against the possibility of fire in enclosed engine compartments and so the fuel lines will normally be in metal, probably copper, and the flexible section connecting the line to the engine will be in braided reinforced hose.

For electrical systems, dual batteries will be required, both being charged by the same engine-mounted alternator; one being used for engine starting purposes and the other being used to supply auxiliary circuits. A paralleling switch will also be included into the circuit which allows both batteries to be put on line for engine starting in case the starting battery is low; in this way you can ensure a high degree of reliability in the electrical system. All electrical wiring needs to be permanently installed and very carefully secured and routed to avoid the possibility of chafe. This particularly applies to the main battery leads where, if a short circuit occurs, the resulting heat could rapidly start a fire.

The auxiliary circuits need to be protected with fuses or breakers but if breakers are used they must be the type which will stand up to the high dynamic loadings of a rigid inflatable, and not simply pop out at the slightest excuse. Although water shouldn't get into the engine compartment, a certain amount of spray or damp is inevitable so connections should be well protected against corrosion by spraying with silicone grease or other proprietary products. All connections should be positive bolted connections rather than push fit connectors which have a nasty habit of jumping loose just when you least want them to. The highest possible standard of electrical outfitting is essential in a rigid inflatable and this is not an area for making economies.

The batteries represent a considerable weight and as previously described, they should be bolted down against a firm surface and not just lashed in position. Not only will you lose your electrical circuits if they should work lose, but you have the double problems of acid corrosion and possibly a fire if they come adrift. The batteries should be installed where they can be accessible for easy maintenance and inspection.

COOLING AND EXHAUST SYSTEMS

The cooling system on diesel engines needs to be engineered very carefully with the best materials, bearing in mind that any failure could result in sea water pouring into the boat. Whilst it is unlikely to cause the boat to sink because of the inherent buoyancy in the RIB, it will almost certainly incapacitate the boat. The water piping should be of the best quality and where flexible sections are introduced to the piping, these should be fitted with double worm-drive clips and carried through in strong reinforced hose. The pipework should be adequately secured against movement and both the seacock and the fuel shut off valve should be accessible from outside the engine compartment so that they can be rapidly operated in an emergency. Similarly the electrical main switch should be outside the engine compartment, so that it can be easily reached in the event of a fire.

Normally, a wet exhaust system is fitted to rigid inflatables. The engine cooling water is injected into the exhaust to silence it, but more importantly to cool the hot gases so that they can pass safely through the reinforced rubber hose which comprises the exhaust. Here again you have a potential source of fire, because if this cooling water stops either through a faulty water pump or drive, or through a hose failure, then within a matter of seconds the hot exhaust gases can melt the rubber pipe and set fire to it. Here you have a compounding situation where not only is the cooling water flooding into the engine compartment through the broken pipe but the engine exhaust is also on fire. With luck, the flooding water might just put out the engine exhaust fire, but the chances are that you have quite a serious situation on your hands which needs to be dealt with promptly. The problem is that a failure in the cooling water will not quickly show on the engine water temperature gauge or in the alarm system when you have a heat exchanger and fresh water cooling, as is found on most modern diesels. To guard against this situation you need a flow alarm in the cooling water system which will immediately indicate if the water flow has stopped. The sensor needs to be carefully positioned because failure in a hose may not sound the warning alarm if water is still flowing through the pipe. Probably the best position for such a sensor is close to where the cooling water passes into the exhaust pipe.

Apart from the problems of hose failure, you need to make sure that water cannot flow back down through the exhaust and into the engine when the boat is going astern or is stopped in a seaway. When going astern, the engine exhaust pressure will normally keep water out of the exhaust pipe; the biggest worry is when the boat is stopped dead in the water. The solution here is to take the exhaust upwards before it runs down to the transom, or at least have the outlet manifold, where the rubber section connects in, close to the highest point in the engine compartment and certainly well above the water line.

VENTILATING THE ENGINE COMPARTMENT

Ventilation is the other important aspect for an inboard diesel engine. You need to combine a system which will allow plenty of air to enter the engine compartment, but at the same time keep water out. A simple louvered vent is generally all that is required and if it is placed in a protected area around the console, this will ensure that relatively dry air gets to the engine compartment. A water trap can be incorporated into the system so that if water does get into the intake it will settle out. The air intake should be positioned close to the bottom of the engine compartment because incoming cool air will then rise naturally and the dual purpose of feeding the engine with air for combustion as well as maintaining reasonably even temperatures in the engine compartment.

Boats which have a capsize reversal system also need to have the engine modified to cope adequately with a capsize. Both exhaust and air intake will need some form of temporary sealing arrangement to prevent water getting into the engine whilst the boat is upside down. As far as the intake is concerned, extending this into the bilges is normally adequate, because any water in the intake will be well below the level at the point at which the intake exits into the engine compartment when it is upside down. A ball valve system is usually incorporated into the exhaust pipe to prevent water running back up the exhaust pipe. A mercury switch is fitted to ensure that the engine cuts out when it is upside down. Apart from preventing the propeller from turning in mid air, this also stops the engine damaging itself when the lubricating oil runs down from the sump on to the pistons. Much the same approach is adopted when outboard motors are used, but here the engine hood also has to be sealed to prevent water ingress. Given the right level of attention, there is no reason why the engine shouldn't start again when the boat is righted, although for a starter to work, the sealed type of batteries are necessary and particular attention needs to be paid to the waterproofing on the electrical system, certainly as far as engine starting is concerned.

Propulsion systems

Outboard propulsion is almost entirely with a propeller. However there are water jet versions of outboards on the market which can be a viable alternative for inflatables and are an option worth considering. With inboard engines, the main choice lies between a stern drive and a water jet. The stern drive is somewhat similar to the bottom end of an outboard motor but the drive is taken through two right angles to get to the propeller. Because the drive is hinged at the top joint, the angle can be adjusted by a power trim system which is a useful benefit when driving the boat in different conditions. This same system can be used to tilt the engine right up when putting a rigid inflatable on to a launching trailer. Modern units are very robust and can adequately take the stress and strain of RIB performance.

Both outboards and stern drives can be trimmed to optimise the angle of propeller thrust and this in turn will adjust the trim of the boat. On smaller outboards, probably up to 50 hp, the adjustment is manual and can only be done when the boat is stopped. A pin which links the outboard leg to the mounting bracket can be fitted into a series of holes to make the adjustment. On larger outboards and with most stern drives, power trim is fitted. Here an hydraulic cylinder is used to alter the angle of the leg and this enables the trim to be adjusted underway using a dashboard switch. With trim, when the leg is moved out the bow tends to rise. Move the leg in and the bow drops.

With outboards and stern drives, the propeller pitch needs to be adjusted to the performance of the boat. Delivered new, the boat will prob-ably have been trialled and a suitable propeller fitted. The main reasons for changing from the standard propeller could include: wanting better accel-eration for water skiing, carrying a heavy load such as a team of divers or if you simply want a more responsive boat where top speed is not so important. In all these cases a smaller pitch propeller will improve things, but you have to be careful not to select one which is too small or the engine could over-rev if the throttle is wound wide open. With an rpm gauge you can see what is happening to the engine but without one you will need to be cautious about fitting a smaller pitch propeller. In most cases, you will only need to go down 1 inch on the pitch to get the desired improvement.

WATER JETS
The main benefit of the more expensive water jet systems is the lack of any protruding parts below the bottom of the boat, which makes them a safer proposition for picking up casualties or divers from the water. Water jets do tend to be heavier units and the handling of a boat with this propulsion system does take some getting used to, although once mastered, the handling characteristics are superior to those of a propeller-driven boat. The water jet is also largely immune to debris in the water and gives you a lot more freedom of operation in very shallow water conditions. Perhaps the biggest advantage of a water jet is its ability to absorb a wide variety of boat loading conditions and it is rarely as critical as a propeller system.

With a stern drive unit, a gear box is required, but this may be incorpor-ated directly into the top of the stern drive itself. Alternatively, the gear box can be mounted directly on to the engine to give ahead, neutral and astern. With a water jet, there is no reason why a gear box should be required except to help match the engine speed to that required by the water jet. However having a reverse facility on the water jet can be use-ful to back flush the water jet if debris is ingested and a neutral capabil-ity is also useful to allow the engine to be run independent of the water jet for warming up and/or tuning. Some water jets use rubber cutless type bearings for the drive shaft and these bearings do not take kindly to being run dry. Therefore when a rigid inflatable is launched from a mother ship the engine needs to be warmed up prior to launching, the water jet either has to be isolated from the diesel or it has to have bearings which can be run without water lubrication; also the sea water pump should be of a type which can be run dry, ie it should be a gear pump rather than the rubber impeller type. As we have seen, the rubber exhaust system will not take kindly to running dry and so if this arrangement is required, then a dry metal exhaust system needs to be used to replace the rubber flexible hose. An alternative is to have a water connection from a hose on to the sea water cooling system so that water will continue to circulate through the system even when the engine is run out of water.

TWIN ENGINES
With twin engines and twin drives you get a higher degree of reliability in as much as the boat can still operate or at least get home on one engine. With outboards, it might just be possible for the boat to get up on to the plane when running on one engine of a twin engine rig, although it will probably be necessary to change the propeller to a smaller pitch to achieve this. With a twin diesel engine installation, the chances of getting the boat up on to the plane with just one engine running are very small but at least if the second engine keeps running you have a 'get-you-home' facility, albeit at slow speed. It is rare to use a twin-engined capability for close quarters manoeuvring, such as putting one engine ahead and one astern for tight turning. The rigid inflatable is generally so highly manoeuverable that this facility is not required and the main advantage of having twin engines is that even with failure of one engine or drive, you can still keep going. If you are going to achieve this successfully then it is important that the systems for each engine are isolated as far as possible, so that the engines operate off separate fuel tanks, electrical and cooling systems. If you want the ultimate in self-sufficiency then you might even consider

A large rescue rigid inflatable which is diesel water jet powered and has a fully enclosed wheelhouse.

developing the systems so that the tank for one engine can be switched over to supply the other or both engines. The same can be done with the electrical system, but you have to be a bit careful not to take this interchangeability too far because the more complex the systems, the more chance there is for something to go wrong.

It is perhaps better to concentrate on making the basic installations reliable. This is the real key to RIB or inflatable boat reliability. Even with a small yacht tender you have to appreciate that you are far more at risk when you take to the tender than you are when staying on board the mother ship; going ashore in an inflatable and suffering an engine failure could get you into serious trouble quite quickly if you are blown out to sea. It is amazing how much you take an engine which is running for granted, but if you have ever experienced the eerie silence which follows an engine failure at sea, then you will have learned the hard way by experience, that installing and maintaining engine systems to a high standard, is one of the essentials for safe boating.

CHAPTER 5

FITTINGS AND EQUIPMENT

The basic concept of an inflatable is one of simplicity, an elemental boat which is extremely functional. There is, however, always a strong temptation with any boat to add fixtures, fittings and equipment and it can be easy to justify each individual item. But if you are not careful, the boat ends up getting heavier and more cluttered, and the concept of simplicity is quickly lost. There is certain basic equipment that you must carry on board mainly in the interests of safety and security, and there is a great deal of potentially useful equipment that you could carry on board but none of which comes into the category of the essential. As the owner of an inflatable or a RIB, you must ask yourself what equipment you need to carry on board, bearing in mind that you must find stowage for it, something that is not always easy on this type of boat.

The best way to approach equipping an inflatable or RIB is to divide equipment into two categories: the essentials and the desirables. You have no choice about essentials apart from deciding on the quantity of any item you carry on board. With the desirables, the choices may vary, depending on what you are going to use the boat for on a particular day. For instance, if you are going fishing then a bait box and rod stowage may be an essential part of the equipment. If you are going diving, then air bottle stowage is equally important. When deciding on what equipment to carry on board, it is worth looking at the approach used by the professionals. They carry very little superfluous equipment, just the necessary essentials; equally importantly, every piece of equipment has its own dedicated stowage so that it can't rattle around inside the boat, and it is accessible for immediate use when required. Stowage is probably one of the most difficult things to achieve satisfactorily on these boats, so when considering equipment, look at the stowage factors first.

Stowage of equipment

On the small inflatable yacht tender there is no stowage space at all built into the boat, so the best solution is to have a waterproof bag for essential items. These inflatables only really need the bare essentials of safety equipment, perhaps a couple of flares, a torch and bellows. Even when these inflatables are only used in harbours, it is possible to get into trouble in

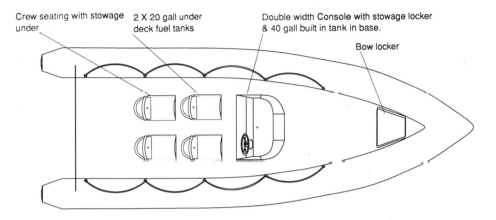

Crew seating with stowage under.

2 X 20 gall under deck fuel tanks

Double width Console with stowage locker & 40 gall built in tank in base.

Bow locker

Typical layout of a large rigid inflatable with full width console and individual seats for the crew, the handhold on the rear of the seats providing a grip for the crewman behind.

strong winds or through other circumstances, and when using the boat at night time, the torch is essential. If you keep your waterproof equipment bag permanently packed it could also double up as an emergency grab bag if the inflatable is ever needed for an emergency role.

For larger inflatables, an equipment bag is usually fitted to the tubes under the bow canopy to provide storage for safety equipment. What you carry on board here will depend a great deal on how you use the boat, but the bare minimum mentioned for the inflatable yacht tender is equally applicable. Ideally, the stowage bag should be waterproof because you may wish to leave the equipment permanently on board so it is important that it does not deteriorate. Waterproof zips can provide the solution for sealing the opening in the storage bag, but the more common type of bag used simply has a flap held down by Velcro which is certainly not watertight. If this is the case you should make sure that there are two or three holes in the bottom of the bag so that any water can drain away. It is a good idea to check the contents regularly for signs of corrosion or water damage.

An alternative to a bag is a stowage box which fits either under the bow canopy, or in the stern alongside the transom. A box made from moulded rubber or plastic which has a degree of give will be better than a completely rigid box. There is a great tendency to just pile equipment inside a box or bag and think that it is secure. The stowage needs to be carefully organised so that loose equipment doesn't rattle around and get damaged when the boat is at sea. Equipment inside a built-in pouch is rubbing against the air tube when the boat is bouncing at sea possibly causing chafe and even a puncture.

On a rigid inflatable there is more scope to build in efficient watertight stowage; this can take the form of a bow compartment or locker under the console or seats. Again it is important that any equipment put in the stowages is firmly secured so that it doesn't rattle around inside and get damaged. It is generally the hard items such as torches and flares which cause a problem, so they should be stowed underneath elastic straps so that they can't move.

Safety equipment

FLARES

Every inflatable, whether used in harbour or out in the open sea, should carry a couple of flares to call for assistance in an emergency. In harbour, an incident can happen when you least expect it, perhaps someone falling overboard and you are unable to row back to them against the wind, or the engine may fail and you find yourself drifting with wind and tide. To cope with an inshore emergency of this type, a couple of red hand flares will probably be adequate to summon help because in a harbour there are usually plenty of people looking at the water, so that your flare will rapidly attract attention. If you go out to sea, whether it is just a coastal run or out into open water away from land, then the hand flare is still effective, but you will want something more persistent. You should supplement the hand flares with a couple of parachute flares. These are fired up into the air to a height of 1000 feet and are effective both day and night over a wide range. Their big advantage is that they burn for 30 or 40 seconds which makes them much more likely to be spotted. Two flares of this type should be considered to be the bare minimum. They are expensive items, but if you do get into trouble at sea then two flares may not be enough to summon the help that you desperately need. A larger vessel will normally carry at least six of these parachute flares and, in my view, three should be considered the bare minimum to give you a reasonable chance of summoning help in the open sea.

Smoke flares are often suggested as part of the equipment to be carried but they are not usually visible over a long distance except in still conditions where the smoke is not dispersed quickly by the wind. They also tend to be much larger than the hand or parachute flares and of course they are only effective in the day time and not at night. We will look at this question of flares in more detail in the chapter on safety and survival, but the most important point is that they are stowed very securely in the boat with no chance of movement. They will deteriorate very quickly if they are allowed to bounce around and there is also the possibility that they may go off inadvertently if they suffer this sort of abuse.

VHF RADIO

A much more effective way of calling for help in an emergency is a VHF radio working on the marine band. There are now waterproof hand-held VHF radios on the market and whilst the waterproof versions are considerably more expensive than the non-waterproof type, they are ideal for a

RIB or inflatable. With a radio, you can let people know what the problem is, and your position and, most importantly, from your point of view, you will know, when you get a reply, that someone has received your message. The waterproof radio can be just as effective in the inflatable yacht tender both as a means of regular communication with the mother vessel and for emergency use. Whilst they are generally very robustly constructed, hand-held VHFs need to be stowed carefully; one of the best stowages is in a secure pocket on personal clothing, so that even if the boat capsizes and you end up in the water, you can still call for help. Your body will also help to protect the radio from violent movement and hard knocks.

The non-waterproof VHF sets are much cheaper but they are also more vulnerable and you will need to protect them carefully. The best type of protection is in a purpose-made waterproof plastic bag, preferably one which will allow you to operate the radio without taking it out of the cover. We take a look later in Chapter 7 at alternative types of radio which can be permanently installed in the boat, but certainly these days a radio is generally considered to be essential equipment in any inflatable or RIB.

ANCHORS
It is wise to make yourself as self-sufficient as possible when you go to sea in an inflatable or RIB; this means being able to sort out problems as they arise rather than having to call for help at the slightest sign of trouble. Another essential piece of equipment which should be on board is an anchor, and apart from its obvious use when you want to stop and go for a swim or enjoy the scenery, the anchor is also an important piece of safety equipment. Its main use is to prevent you from drifting while you

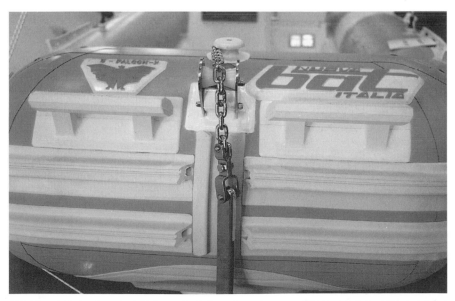

A comprehensive bow installation with fittings for using an anchor and chain. The moulded rubber handholds double up as cleats for mooring.

are trying to fix your engine or at least stop in comparative safety until someone can come out to tow you back into harbour. An anchor used for this emergency role will have to be effective and have good holding power under adverse conditions. You will need an anchor of adequate weight, with sufficient length of line. The best place to stow it is securely strapped down to the wooden decking or floor boards where it can't come in contact with the inflatable tube. Ideally the anchor should have a short length of chain about 2 metres or so, between the anchor and the rope anchor line to increase the holding power of the anchor; any connecting shackles in the line should be securely moused to prevent the screw pins coming undone when the anchor is in use.

There is a wide choice of anchors to choose from and you have to balance the holding power of the different types against the ability to stow them comfortably inside the rigid inflatable. Anchors such as the Danforth are probably the lightest in weight when compared with their holding power, and they have the advantage that they stow flat which makes it easier to find a home for them on board. The Danforth is very effective in sand and mud, but generally less effective on a rocky bottom which is where you may end up in an emergency. The Bruce and CQR anchors are heavier and less easy to stow, but tend to have excellent holding power. The old fashioned Fisherman's anchor will stow virtually flat and it probably has the best holding power on a rocky bottom, but to be effective it needs to be fairly heavy. Finally, there are folding anchors, which seem like a good idea from the stowage angle but these are rarely as robust as their non-folding counterparts. When you need an anchor in an emergency you generally need it very badly, and so reliability should be your primary consideration. For use on an inflatable, the anchor which best fulfils the criteria of good holding, reasonable weight and stowability is probably the Danforth.

The anchor line should be long enough to put out an effective scope in an emergency; 30 metres should be the minimum length. This anchor line can also make an effective tow line, and it should be of adequate strength to take the whole weight of the boat in extreme conditions. You will need a secure fastening point for the anchor line in the boat. In a RIB a strong mooring post is possible in the bow but on an inflatable there will only be a metal towing ring fixed at the bow so the line should be passed through the ring and fixed inboard. A bridle fixed to two points will help to take the strain. Make sure that the rope does not chafe the tube as it leads over the bow.

A sea anchor is often suggested as an important piece of safety equipment on inflatable boats. It is designed to prevent the boat drifting when not under power and it can also be used to keep the boat's head up into the sea which can make the motion more comfortable, particularly if you have to work on the engine in an emergency. You can use the sea anchor to reduce drift if you are blowing down on to a lee shore, but to be effective, the anchor has to be of adequate size and to have a reasonably strong line attached to it. The sea anchor often found on inflatables and RIBs is the type designed for use in liferafts. These may be adequate for the small inflatable yacht tender, but anything larger will need something stronger, and more robust.

TORCHES

The final item of essential safety equipment is a torch. Even if you are not planning to operate the boat at night, you may find yourself overtaken by darkness, perhaps through an engine failure or adverse weather conditions. Not only does the torch give you a light to effect engine repairs or to check charts, but it also doubles as an emergency navigation light. The only type of torch worth considering in an inflatable or RIB is a waterproof one, and there is a wide variety of these available on the market. Once again, stowage for the torch is important if it is going to survive and it should be checked at regular intervals to make sure that it continues to function. You might consider carrying spare batteries and bulb on board because you want to make sure that it will definitely work when you most need it.

Other important equipment

There are many other items of equipment, some of which could be considered in the category of 'essential', but a great deal will depend on how you use the boat. Whilst you may not need a first aid kit in the inflatable yacht tender, you should consider this as part of the inventory for inflatables and RIBs. The risk of injury in these boats when driven hard at sea is considerable so you really need a basic first aid kit. The sort of injury that you may have to treat could be cuts or possibly broken limbs and so you will need some plasters, wound dressings and a couple of triangular bandages. Splints would be useful but you can probably improvise those from other equipment on board or use other parts of the body to immobilise an arm or a leg. You could also include pain killers, but any that are strong enough to be effective when someone is injured usually require a doctor's permission but aspirin may be helpful with some conditions. Make sure that your first aid kit can cope with the immediate situation and then either call for help or get the casualty ashore as soon as possible.

COMPASSES

A compass is another item of equipment which should be considered essential in all but the smallest inflatable. If you undertake serious navigation when you can be out of sight of land, then the compass is a vital navigation tool for steering a consistent course or when caught out in fog. You can usually keep a steady course in relation to wind or waves, but often fog will occur in flat calm conditions when you have no other sense of direction except with a compass. For the get-you-home situation, you are probably best off with a small hand-bearing compass, either of the magnetic or electronic type which can be stowed away. The hand-held electronic type is among the most compact compasses on the market, yet despite its small size, this pocket sized unit is very effective and can also be carried on a string round your neck.

If you are navigating seriously and using the compass to steer courses well out of sight of land, then something more permanent is required; most rigid inflatables fitted with a console have a proper compass installation. The compass should be of a type which is specifically designed for high speed operations; this usually involves giving the compass very heavy damping so that the card doesn't jump around and become unintelligible in rough seas. Bear in mind, when installing the compass, that it can be affected by other instruments in its vicinity, particularly tachometers and electronics. Whilst it is not suggested that you go to the trouble of having the compass fully corrected by a compass adjuster, it does pay to check it to make sure that there are no glaring inconsistencies in the readings. Checking can be done by using a hand-bearing compass, either of the magnetic or electronic type, held well away from any possible magnetic interference; the courses are then compared. This should be done both with the engine running and with it stopped. Also, check it with the electronics switched on and off so that you know what effect each instrument is having on the compass. Magnetic interference can vary so check the reading on a variety of headings. If you do find a difference between the reading of a hand-bearing compass and the installed compass, assume that the hand-bearing compass is giving the correct magnetic heading and you will be able to work out the correction to apply to the steering compass.

You can also get an electronic steering compass. The big advantage here is that the heading sensor can be installed remote from the display, enabling you to site it away from most magnetic influence. It is not easy to find a suitable location for this sensor unit, which should be well clear of engines, fuel tanks and other steel items. You would certainly have to be careful about installing it in a locker where magnetic items such as an anchor or torch could be stowed in close proximity without you being aware of the problem. The forward part of the boat may be reasonably free from magnetic influences but here the motion can be quite severe which is not conducive to producing steady compass readings.

With the electronic compass, you can mount the display at any angle and in any position so that it can be optimised for easy steering; you can also select the type of compass display that suits your requirements. Most of these units offer the alternative of a digital or a 360° display and the digital type of compass heading is surprisingly easy to steer with.

Some units have the option of having an off-course indicator which means that once the boat is settled on its course you press the appropriate button and the display shows whether you are to port or starboard of the selected course enabling you to make the necessary steering correction. With this type of display you don't have to read any numbers and a quick glance will be enough to tell you what course correction is required. This means that you can concentrate on watching the waves ahead rather than the compass itself, making it an excellent steering indicator for small fast boats.

TOOLS AND SPARES

Engine tools and spares are essential on any inflatable or RIB fitted with an engine. There is nothing more frustrating than engine failure at sea, when you know what is wrong but haven't got the equipment on board to fix it. Most engine failures can be attributed to the fuel supply or the electrical system so carry appropriate spares and tools for basic repairs to these two systems. Select general purpose tools such as adjustable spanners, screwdrivers and pliers. If you can afford it, these should be made of stainless steel which won't corrode in the marine environment.

If your boat has an outboard motor then always keep a plug spanner and a spare set of sparking plugs on board because it is much easier to replace a plug than to try and clean an existing one. There is probably not a lot you can do at sea to repair electrical problems but for electric starts a manual starting cord may help you out of a tight spot.

For the fuel system, carry worm drive clips; a spare length of flexible fuel pipe can be useful provided you also have some small lengths of rigid tube with which to connect them in. The flexible sections of fuel lines which can be vulnerable to damage as can the connections. Spare O rings for the connection seals are also useful spares to carry.

With inboard diesels, the same basic tools and spares are required apart from the sparking plugs. If you have some knowledge of the electrical system, spare fuses and wiring could be handy. A spare impeller for the water pump is worth having on board provided you can get easy access to the pump to replace this item. The most vulnerable part of any diesel engine installation tends to be the electric starter but it is hard to justify carrying a spare for this, and few, if any, high speed diesel engines have any hand starting facility. The main tools you are likely to need is a set of spanners to enable you to bleed air out of the fuel system and the means to clear the fuel filter if this should get blocked.

A spare propeller is a valuable item to carry on board, particularly if you operate the boat off a beach or in shallow water. Whilst on the question of spares, if the boat is operated regularly at night, spare bulbs for navigation lights are important items and, of course, fuses for the auxiliary circuits are equally essential.

FIRE EXTINGUISHERS

The risk of fire in an inflatable or a RIB is quite small, but you are carrying highly inflammable fuel on board if you have an outboard. There will always be a risk of fire on or around the engine if a fuel line breaks, or the cooling water stops and the engine gets hot. A fire extinguisher may seem like over-kill in an open inflatable when you are surrounded by one of the best firefighting mediums available. The problem is that if you drown an outboard motor with sea water the chances of getting it going again could be quite small. Also it may be difficult to get inside the engine hood to extinguish the fire effectively so a fire extinguisher may be worth its weight one day.

Whilst the dry powder type can be very effective, the powder inside does tend to compact when carried on board a fast boat and so these extinguishers cannot always be relied on to be effective. The Halon fire extinguisher is probably the best, particularly if you have the type where the discharge can be controlled by a trigger mechanism, so that you don't have to fire off all the contents in one shot. Certainly on the large rigid inflatables, where there is a built-in electrical system, then you should certainly consider carrying such a fire extinguisher as part of the on board equipment. Where there is an inboard engine fitted, then some form of permanent fire extinguishing system should be considered for the engine compartment. These come in two forms: an automatic discharge if temperature sensors reach a certain level and a manual discharge which can be activated once you have discovered the fire. There are merits for both systems but, in general, the automatic one is to be preferred, because by the time you have detected a fire in an enclosed compartment, it may have done considerable damage which could prevent you restarting the engine.

The big advantage of a built-in fire extinguishing system is that you don't have to open up the engine hatch to activate it. With a hand system, you have to open up the hatch and this can allow fresh air to rush in and feed the fire which will then flare up and make it much harder to extinguish. This is particularly the case when there is a fuel fire, but you can also get the same effect with an electrical fire where smouldering short-circuiting wires can flare up with a sudden influx of oxygen-rich air.

NAVIGATION LIGHTS

If you plan to operate an inflatable or RIB at night, then navigation lights of one sort or another are required by law. On a small low-speed inflatable, you can get away with simply flashing a torch at any other boat you see on the water, but with the faster type of inflatable and RIB you need something more sophisticated. For small craft under 7 metres the rules only require an all round white light; this is probably adequate for most inflatable boats and smaller RIBs, but with larger rigid inflatables, a proper set of navigation lights is probably the best solution installed on a roll bar or A-frame. You can get away with a single lantern where the port and starboard lights are combined and have the least demand on the battery, but you still need a masthead light and a stern light. Make sure, however, that you carry spare bulbs. All navigation lights need to be fully waterproof and shielded, to a certain extent, to prevent them from destroying your night vision.

Fixtures and accessories

The roll bar is rigged as a permanent fixture in the boat and can be used for a variety of purposes. We have already seen how it provides a useful fixing point for navigation lights and it can provide a similar role for any antennae for radio or navigation electronics. The roll bar can also be used to provide a handhold when working on the engines over the stern, and it is a worthwhile fitting for rigid inflatables which are being used for serious open sea

A police patrol rigid inflatable with self-righting, radar and a towing capability. Note the stern frame to keep the tow rope clear of the outboards. *Photo: Zodiac.*

work. In its simplest form it is a shaped aluminium or stainless steel single tube with flanges to allow it to be bolted on to the deck or the transom.

More substantial A-frames are built up from a set of stainless steel or aluminium tubes usually with two main tubes plus cross-bracing. This type of structure can be designed as a self-righting frame with a mounting point for a capsize reversal air bag and a gas bottle for air bag inflation and operating trigger will also be fastened to the frame.

Any boat needs a means of bailing out water. With inflatable boats it is less easy to engineer a self-draining system, because the deck or floor level is below the waterline except when the boat is planing. Some form of bailer, therefore, should be carried amongst the equipment for this purpose. It can also double as a fire extinguisher by bailing water *into* the boat, and it can also be a useful item when you are working on the engine, for holding dismantled parts so that they don't get lost on the floor or fall overboard.

Boat manufacturers offer a wide range of accessories which allow you to adapt the boat for your specific requirements. There is considerable merit in buying equipment from the manufacturer's range of accessories simply because you know that it will be compatible with the boat and there will be few if any problems in fitting and using it. On top of the basic specification of the boat you can add such items as bow dodgers, windscreens and even roll bars and frames. Oars or paddles will also be provided with a compatible stowage and rowlocks where necessary.

Within the range of standard accessories there will often be items for specialised use. Bait tanks, for instance, will be needed by a fisherman to keep bait alive and active. These are generally fitted with a small electric pump and suction and discharge pipes to circulate sea water through them. Obviously you will also need a battery to power the pump, and

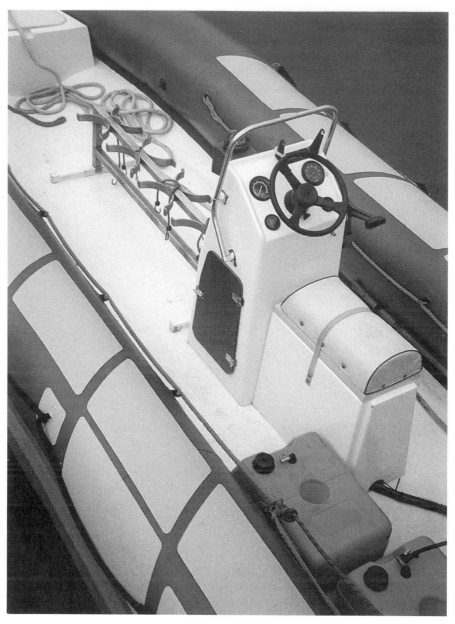

A diving RIB with bottle rack forward and console sited further aft. Distribution of weight on dive boats is critical to enable them to plane effectively. Plastic fuel tanks are used in this boat and they should be well secured.

specialised tanks which are supplied as self-contained units are available. The logical place for suction and discharge is over the transom and such bait tanks are only viable when operating at slow speeds although they could be effective on RIBs at higher speeds because there is a firm floor on which to mount the tank.

Weather protection on an inflatable helps to keep both boat and crew dry and could be used to convert the boat into a camping unit. *Photo: Novamarine.*

Similarly, the divers need racks to secure their air bottles. These allow the bottles to be stowed upright where they are readily available for use but securely stowed when the boat is travelling to the diving area at speed. Diving boats are usually fitted with extra handholds along the tubes so that the divers can hold on securely and enable them to re-enter the boat easily after a dive.

If the boat is used as a bathing platform, some form of boarding ladder is useful. It is possible to get on board by simply climbing in over the tube but you need to be reasonably athletic for this and it is not always easy if you are tired after a swim. Whilst a rigid ladder of this type does the job very effectively, it is not necessarily the easiest thing to stow on board when it is not in use. Folding rigid ladders are available which can make a good compromise solution. With a flexible type of ladder you find your feet going underneath the boat and it is very hard to climb up in any effective way. It is also possible to get sun canopies which will stay in position even at relatively fast speeds, sun beds for sun bathing and all the requirements of leisure at sea.

There is really no limit to the equipment that can be fitted to a rigid inflatable, provided you have the space, and modern electronics are a good example of this. We will be looking at these in a later chapter, particularly with regard to the use of electronic navigation aids.

CHAPTER 6

HANDLING INFLATABLES

The techniques for handling inflatable boats on the water can be very different from those of conventional craft of a similar size. This particularly applies to both yacht tenders and the smaller powered inflatables. The handling of rigid inflatables is more akin to that of a similar sized sports boat but still has its unique features. For the purposes of this chapter we will divide inflatables and RIBs into three separate categories: first the small, flat-bottomed yacht tender powered by oars or a small outboard motor; secondly, the relatively flat-bottomed inflatable which operates at planing speeds and is fitted with a more powerful motor; and thirdly the rigid inflatable which may come in a variety of sizes but where the handling techniques for the deep vee hull are very much the same.

Inflatable yacht tenders

In this category are included inflatables which have the tube going all the way round the boat, ie those without a solid transom inserted into the hull, and also flat-bottomed inflatables fitted with a transom but are only designed to accept a low-powered outboard motor and which are primarily aimed at the yacht tender market.

The flat or nearly flat bottom of the simply-constructed yacht tender inflatable gives it virtually no grip on the water. These boats can skate sideways at the slightest provocation under the influence of wind or other external forces and you need a firm hand to control them if you are going to make any progress. Your first indication that these inflatables have a will of their own comes as you try and step into the boat – it will try and slide sideways away from you making it a tricky business trying to get in without getting wet.

Ideally, get someone else to hold the boat and step right into it rather than on the inflatable tube using the tubes for support. Even once you are in, standing up can be hazardous as any slight imbalance will jerk the boat sideways rendering you liable to be tipped into the water.

It seems amazing that boats with such characteristics ever became acceptable in the yacht market, but they replaced wooden or fibreglass dinghies which could be equally unstable when you tried to step into them. Also they were far less forgiving when alongside the shiny topsides of a yacht. With care and practice boarding can be mastered but it is essential to keep a hold of the yacht or the jetty from which you are stepping and gradually transfer your weight into the inflatable, rather than take a sudden leap.

ROWING AN INFLATABLE

With a flat-bottomed inflatable in these smaller sizes you need to remember that every time you move in one direction, the inflatable will want to go in the other as a reaction to your movement. You can harness this behaviour to good effect when you are rowing, but the techniques are quite different from those used with a conventional rowing boat. When you stop pulling on the oars in an inflatable the boat virtually stops dead in the water and it carries no way. Because it has no bite on the water it will be influenced by the wind. So if you are rowing in a fresh breeze, then it is better to take short, sharp pulls on the oars, to keep the boat moving in the desired direction, rather than the long, slow pulls that you would normally use on a conventional rowing boat. Short, sharp pulls also require less room for the rower, which can be useful when you are carrying a load of equipment for the yacht or have a couple of passengers on board.

In calmer conditions you can row the inflatable with longer strokes which makes rowing any distance more comfortable. In either case, you need to balance the pull on the oars because these small inflatables have virtually no directional stability and will spin round if the pull on one oar is stronger than the other – a technique which takes a fair amount of practice and perseverance!

If the inflatable has moulded rubber rowlocks, these tend to grip the oars as they swivel, and they have a nasty habit of trying to turn the oar, making it difficult to grip the handle hard enough to row effectively. A simple solution is to spray the inner edge of the rowlock with a silicone lubricant so that the oar can move much more freely inside the rowlock aperture.

In calm, or near calm, waters there is no problem in handling one of these small inflatable boats once you get used to the technique, but in stronger winds or waves you need to exercise much more care. You may find yourself making little or no headway against the wind and being blown down wind. For a yacht at a mooring where the jetty is down wind it can pay to try rowing upwind when you leave the yacht just to make sure you can make effective progress when you want to return. An alternative might be to follow the shore line from the jetty in more protected waters when you leave to come back, so that you get to a point abeam, or even upwind, of the yacht before you set out on the open water journey back. Trying to row upwind in a fresh breeze in a small inflatable can be a very unrewarding experience; you can find yourself getting very tired long before you get anywhere near your destination. As soon as you stop rowing to have a breather, the boat takes off down wind again, and you lose a lot of the ground you have already gained. The solution is always to think carefully about the return trip before you set out in one of these inflatables.

Rowing in waves can be equally difficult. The uneven surface of the water can make it much harder to row effectively and if you miss your grip with one oar then the boat immediately spins round and again you lose ground. These small inflatables can also be very wet, as water and spray tends to follow the curve of the tube and come in over the bow so it is better to put any cargo or passengers towards the stern of the boat. This also helps to keep the bow out of the water and enables it to lift more readily to the oncoming waves. The boat itself is quite safe and will not sink, but if you do take water on board, then it becomes even harder to row, although there is the compensating effect that at least the drift of the boat downwind will be reduced.

FITTING A SMALL ENGINE

You should restrict journeys in small inflatables to short distances in the sheltered waters of the harbour and in winds of under force 4 otherwise you will have difficulty in controlling both the boat and the direction in which you are heading. One solution is to fit a bracket over the tube on which a small outboard engine can be mounted. These inflatables are so easily driven that you only need an engine of 1 or 2 horsepower to make progress in reasonable conditions. One of the main problems you might experience is in engine starting because petrol engines of this size are invariably hand started. The sharp pull you need on the starter cord can be enough to make you lose your balance, particularly if the engine has to be started in gear causing the boat to move ahead as soon as the engine fires. You should be able to start the engine from a seated position; once underway be ready to steer the boat in the intended direction. With one person helming from the stern the bow will be lifted adequately to cope with small waves but luggage and passengers will have to be carefully arranged to trim the boat to give a reasonably dry ride and good progress. Also you will need to adjust your speed to match the conditions. A bow dodger will help to give a dry ride and keep luggage and stores dry when ferrying between boat and shore. If, however, you think that you can avoid getting wet in an inflatable, one trip will soon put you straight. Any water in the bottom of the boat will immediately collect around your shoe as you step into the boat – it will run to the deepest part of the floor where your weight is concentrated.

If a boat is inflated hard then it will tend to respond more like a hard-hulled boat and this should enhance its performance both under rowing or under power. A boat which is soft and flabby will be harder to row than a fully inflated boat because the rowlocks will bend and twist under the strain. A soft boat will also deform under the weight of people sitting on the tube. Often problems with under-inflation stem from the difficulty of inflating the boat on the deck of the yacht or when alongside, especially when the temperature may be moderately high. The pressure may be fine on deck but as soon as the boat is afloat, the cooler water effectively reduces the pressure inside the tubes and you get a flabby boat. The boat may have been towed astern before use and it is very hard to add extra air to the tubes when it is moored alongside as there is no firm platform on which to put the bellows. Hard inflation of inflatables certainly helps the handling, but do remember that if they are left out in hot sun the pressure can rise to unacceptably high levels.

Powered inflatables.

The smaller yacht type of inflatable relies entirely on the inflatable air tubes to give it size and dimension. At the same time this limits the power which these craft can handle because there is very little longitudinal stiffness to take the thrust of the engine, causing the tubes to buckle under the strain of higher engine power. Inflatable boats designed to take larger outboard engines, and to operate as planing boats, require additional stiffness in the form of wooden, fibreglass or aluminium floor-boards which link into a wooden or fibreglass transom. With these rigid floors inserted into the boat it is possible to use wood or inflatable keels to help shape and tension the bottom of the boat to produce a better planing surface. Even so the keel tends to have a very shallow vee bottom giving handling characteristics which are very different from any other type of boat on the market. These inflatable boats still rely on the tubes to give the boat shape and character; the rigid components of the boat are rarely rigid throughout the length of the craft so that the essential flexibility of the inflatable boat is retained. This gives the variable geometry characteristics of the inflatable which we talked about in the introduction. To a certain extent, the relatively flat bottom shape of these boats, which would be expected to give a very hard impact when operating in waves, is cushioned by the ability of the inflatable tubes to deform and absorb some of the shock. Compared with the equivalent sized sportsboat, the inflatable tends to have a much flatter bottom, a blunter entry due to its rounded bow, and a wider beam/length ratio. All these characteristics have considerable influence on the handling characteristics of the boat.

HANDLING CHARACTERISTICS

Inflatable boats tend to be generally very seaworthy which is partly due to the fact that they are virtually unsinkable, but also to the fact that the tubes can deform and shape themselves to the waves. This, combined with quick acceleration and high degree of manoeuvrability gives an inflatable boat an acceptable performance in sea conditions which an equivalent sports boat might find very daunting. The excellent manoeuvrability is largely due to the fact that the boats have a very flat bottom section with a maximum vee at the transom of 5 degrees providing very little lateral resistance in the water. Turning the wheel or the tiller produces an immediate response, therefore, and the boat can turn very, very quickly indeed. However, over-enthusiastic use of the tiller or wheel can cause the propeller to operate just below the surface of the water giving it very little 'bite'. This means that the engine loses thrust until you close the throttle, allowing the propeller to bite again before gradually reopening the throttle. When operating in rough sea conditions, this can take up to 5 seconds which could be a critical time to lose control and the essential acceleration to power away from a breaking wave from astern. So, really tight turns should be avoided. The tiller steering on lower-powered outboards can lead to over-enthusiastic manoeuvres because the tiller can be moved to the 'hard over' position very easily; care is therefore necessary with tiller steering to prevent this reaction.

DRIFTING
The flat-bottomed characteristic of the inflatable hull will make it very susceptible to sideways drift. This has to be carefully considered when the engine is stopped; under the influence of a fresh breeze, a boat will make quite rapid progress perhaps at the rate of two or three knots down to leeward. The main danger here is that if you stop, perhaps to check the engine or fuel, you can find yourself drifting to leeward quite rapidly and possibly into danger. If you stop at sea for any length of time, perhaps through an engine defect, a sea anchor can reduce the drift quite dramatically and provide greater safety by keeping the boat head to wind.

SLIGHT TO MODERATE SEAS
Under normal conditions, in slight or moderate seas, the inflatable would be driven like any other conventional boat; the steering and throttles being adjusted to keep the boat on course and operating at a comfortable speed. The top speed is rarely more than 25–30 knots, but the ride can feel quite exciting in moderate seas as the boat bounces from wave to wave. This short, sharp movement can make it difficult to use the throttles and to steer smoothly. Quite often the ride comfort can be improved dramatically by only a very minor reduction in speed.

It may look dramatic to power the boat off the top of a wave and land with a great crash on the other side, and for a few waves it can even be quite exciting. However, driving like this puts a very high stress on the boat, particularly on the engine. Remember that if you are driving the boat you can see the waves coming and brace yourself, whereas your crew are much less fortunate; their knuckles will be white trying to hang on, and the initial excitement can quickly turn to apprehension. Often, one of the most highly-stressed areas of an inflatable boat is the engine mountings and the flying and crashing treatment can cause these mountings to crack and break under the very high stress.

Driving the boat with sympathy to the sea conditions means reading the waves ahead and adjusting the speed accordingly. In most conditions in a head sea, you should be able to find a comfortable speed where the boat responds well and can contour the waves, perhaps with the bow leaving the water as you come over the crest but landing on the other side without the boat fully leaving the water; in this way you can make quite comfortable progress to windward. The performance will depend to quite an extent on the size of the boat which you are using and the prevailing sea conditions. If the waves get shorter and steeper, perhaps when wind is against tide, then it may be hard to find a compatible speed. The option here is to turn the boat at an angle to the wind, perhaps 30 or 40°, which effectively lengthens the wave length and reduces the gradient so that you are, to all intents and purposes, tacking across the waves towards your destination. In this kind of short, steep wave, you will often find the crests curling over and breaking, but with the responsiveness of the inflatable, it is usually possible to accelerate and perhaps turn and run along the front of the wave away from the breaking section before you can find a lower part and power across the crest. Despite their apparent regularity when watched from the shore, waves in any particular wave train come in all shapes and sizes, some high, some low, some breaking, some quite smooth and rounded. If you are going to drive at the optimum speed, you need to read these waves and adjust the speed and heading of the boat to take maximum advantage of the immediate conditions.

MODERATE TO ROUGH SEAS

It is in moderate or rough sea conditions that driving skills come into play if you want to make reasonable progress. There will be times when you will come up against a steep wave where there is no way round. The only solution here is to close the throttle and bring the boat down to slow speed to negotiate the wave. Don't be in too much of a hurry to cut the throttle because when you do, the bow will drop and this could be just at the time when you want it to lift up and over the approaching steep wave face. The general solution when driving into head seas is to try and keep the power on and only cut it once the boat has actually started to lift to the wave. In this way, the boat will tend to cut through the crest of the wave and there will be less likelihood of it flying off the top. One thing in favour of inflatable boats is that they have a very quick response to throttle variations and you can use this very effectively in rough seas.

In beam seas it is usually possible to use the full power of the engine in most conditions and make good progress. Inflatables are inherently very stable but you do need to watch out to windward for that occasional big wave with the curling crest which can come along. You may be able to accelerate away and let the wave pass astern of you, or alternatively slow down and let it pass ahead of you, but probably the best solution in these conditions is just to turn away to leeward and keep out of the way of the curling crest until you can drive past clear of it. With experience, you learn to read the waves when you are driving an inflatable and one of the more pleasant sensations is feeling on intimate terms with the sea and the waves, using the boat skilfully to be compatible with the elements rather than trying to fight against them.

TACTICS FOR FOLLOWING SEAS

It may surprise you to know that it is when you are running down wind in an inflatable, in moderate or rough seas, that the boat is at its most

A rigid inflatable about to be overtaken by a heavy breaking wave. Any hesitation here would almost certainly result in a capsize and the only way out is to open the throttle wide. This picture clearly demonstrates why the boat should be capable of travelling faster than the waves.

vulnerable. The main risk here is that you will slow down and let the following seas overtake you. If these following seas happen to be steep and breaking, then there can be a very real risk of broaching and capsizing in this situation. The solution is always to keep the power on with the boat running at least at the speed of the waves. This shouldn't be too difficult even for a comparatively small and low powered inflatable because in inshore waters waves will only travel at around 15 knots whilst in deeper waters they will probably reach 20 knots. These are speeds which should be well within the capabilities of the average inflatable boat. You should be in a position where you can always overtake the waves and drive yourself out of any trouble which may be coming up astern. The bigger the waves the faster they tend to travel. You need to bear this in mind when operating in rough seas where waves can travel up to 25 knots in open water so you should always have a margin of at least 5 knots in hand in excess of the wave speed when travelling in a following sea.

It is very easy to drive over-enthusiastically in a following sea, driving up over the back of a wave only to find that the steeper side of the wave down to leeward leaves the bow of the boat unsupported and you fly off the crest into the unknown. You probably won't come to a lot of harm in an inflatable boat but it may cause it to stop or slow down and then the wave you have just passed over could break on top of you. The best solution, in big waves, is to drive up the back of the wave or the windward side, approaching the crest with caution, and then gradually ease the boat over the crest by applying a bit more throttle. Once over the crest you will probably need to throttle back because the boat is now effectively running

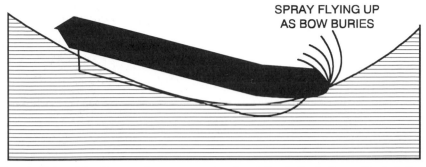

SPRAY FLYING UP
AS BOW BURIES

When the tube at the bow creates a reverse turn in relation to the bottom of the hull, it can generate a great deal of spray when driven over-enthusiastically in a following sea. For best seakeeping, the tube and the hull should have a comfortable interface which allows water to flow smoothly over them.

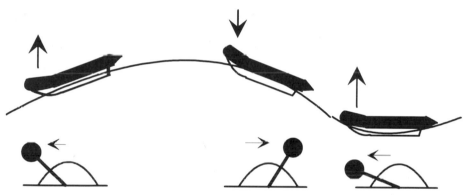

Using throttle control to trim the boat in a head sea. A burst on the throttle as the wave approaches will make the bow lift; closing it will help the bow contour over the top of the wave until the throttle is opened again to lift the bow to the next wave.

down hill and accelerating. If you don't ease back, the boat will plough into the next wave and bury the bow. Again there is probably no serious problem in this, except that you will get covered in a great shower of spray which may temporarily blind you and distract your attention from what is going on behind you, where there could be another curling crest waiting to catch you unawares. If you drive the boat hard in a following sea, you will probably get an exhilarating and dramatic ride for the first few waves, but you will soon find that a gentle hand on the throttle and good concentration on the waves will give a safer and more comfortable passage.

NEGOTIATING HARBOUR BARS

Some of the most dangerous conditions for inflatables can be found on harbour bars. When going out to sea over a harbour bar, the boat is well afloat and the crew should be comfortably organised and well prepared for the very short, steep, breaking waves to come. Inflatable boats can negotiate these conditions if driven carefully but be prepared to ship a lot

of water from these breaking waves. Under these conditions it is useful to
have some form of self-bailing device in the transom to clear this water
automatically. Approach these waves with caution, generally with the
boat off the plane, but with your hand on the throttle ready to accelerate.
As the breaking wave approaches the bow, give a quick burst on the throttle; this serves the dual purpose of lifting the bow under the propeller
thrust but also maintains good directional control so that the approaching
wave does not knock the bow sideways. This burst on the throttle will help
you to power through the breaking wave, but you should cut the throttle
as you come through the crest and drop down the other side. Then be prepared for the same procedure at the next wave.

These breaking waves on a bar can consist of anything from a couple of
breaking waves up to 10 or more depending on the bar conditions. You
should always bear in mind that an engine failure in these conditions is
likely to lead to a fairly quick capsize which may not pose an immediate
threat to life and limb but it certainly puts you into a potentially dangerous situation. Do not attempt to cross a bar unless you have considerable
experience in driving inflatable boats, and you also have confidence in
your boat and equipment so that it can survive the sort of punishment it
will receive. Harbour bars will be at their worst when there is an ebb tide
running out of the harbour meeting a strong wind coming in; also the sea
conditions can often be accentuated on the bar when there is an underly-
ing ground swell coming in. If you have to negotiate the harbour bar in
these conditions then try and find time to study the bar for five or ten minutes before hand. This will often allow you to see areas where the waves
are more moderate and you can use these areas in your passage to open
sea, but beware that what may look like more moderate conditions may in
fact hide shallow water underneath.

LAUNCHING FROM A BEACH
The waves breaking on to a beach can be quite similar to those on a harbour bar – long breaking crests which can present an almost vertical face
to boats trying to get out to sea. Experience with RNLI rescue boats
demonstrates that it is possible to launch boats off an open beach successfully even in very severe conditions but this does require experience and
training. The procedure will depend on the type of beach; probably the
worst conditions for launching is where there is a steep beach with waves
breaking directly on to the shore. This site should be avoided as there is
very little chance of getting the boat into the water with the engine started
without the boat being swamped and washed back on to the shore. On a
more gently shelving beach, the main force of the breakers will be further
out to sea and, whilst the wave motion will still wash in towards the
beach, it will have lost much of its severity, enabling the crew to push the
boat out into deep enough water to get the engine down from its tilted
position and start the engine ready to power out to sea.

Ideally, for beach launching, you want helpers to hold the boat whilst
the crew get on board and the engine is started. Such helpers are likely to

Launching off a beach. The crew have just jumped on board and the boat has cleared the first breaking wave.

get very wet and if there are large breaking waves coming into the beach it can be a tough job trying to hold the bow to seaward while the engine is started. However, at least if there are helpers it gives the crew a chance to get themselves prepared for the white water of the breaking waves; a four or five man team is probably the minimum necessary for this operation. Unless the conditions are very moderate it is almost impossible for one person to hold the boat effectively while the helmsman starts the engine. A three man crew, however, could do the job effectively with two crew members holding the boat on each side whilst the helmsman gets the engine started; once he has got it in gear the two crew have to throw themselves on board and get ready for the breaking waves ahead. It does require team work, practice and co-ordination. Once heading out into the breaking waves, the technique is very similar to that of taking a boat through a harbour bar, but you have very little time to get yourself settled down and organised before having to cope with the breakers.

The boat will often adopt quite frightening angles of pitch when negotiating very steep breaking waves. There appears to be a very real risk of the boat being knocked over backwards but, whilst this looks a possibility, it is an extremely rare occurrence. It is much more likely to capsize sideways, due to the helmsman allowing the bow to wander off so that it is not head to sea. To reduce the risk, the crew should be positioned as far forward in the boat as possible to act as ballast, but it is the hand on the throttle which really controls the attitude of the boat in these conditions.

DRIVING BACK TO SHORE

Coming back in from seaward and having to cope with steep waves on a harbour bar can be more frightening than going out through them. One of the big problems is that you can't really see what the conditions are like until you get in amongst the white water. You need to keep sufficient speed on to be travelling at least at the speed of the waves, preferably slightly faster so that you are slowly overtaking them. The best way to tackle the situation is to ride in on the back of a wave, virtually parking the boat on an upward slope of the wave. Hold it there by delicate throttle control until you sense that the breaker has just curled over and broken on the bar, then you can start to accelerate slowly through the wave and get ready to cope with the next one. The throttle control has to be very gentle and your concentration level very high, because it is easy to find yourself drifting backwards from the crest and then you look astern to see a vertical wall of water towering up right behind you. This is no time for hesitation; you must open the throttle to its full extent and accelerate away from that wave. The idea should be to overtake each wave once it has broken when it will be relatively harmless. If you time it well, your progress through the breaking waves on the bar will be quite quick and precise.

It is much the same when you are coming into a beach but here you have the added problem of having to stop and tilt the engine at the last minute to prevent propeller damage. You drive the boat in over the back of each wave as it breaks, making progress towards the beach; if you are in any doubt about the speed, always open the throttle rather than close it. To close the throttle will almost certainly mean a capsize when the wave behind catches up with you. As you power in towards the beach, the

Landing on an open beach requires skill and co-ordination if there is any surf running.

breaking waves should become smaller and you have to choose your moment very carefully to shut the throttle and quickly tip the engine up so that there is just enough momentum on the boat to take it into the beach without the propeller touching the bottom. As you come into the beach the crew should be ready to jump overboard and turn the boat round head-to the breaking waves, or arrange for helpers to be on hand. On a steeply shelving beach you have very little option but to just drive the boat straight in on to the shore if you need to land at that point. Be aware, however, that such steeply shelving beaches often consist of shingle and the stones may cause damage to the propeller. In any situation where you are coming into a beach, or over a harbour bar, if you are in any doubt about the conditions, then open the throttle rather than close it.

THROTTLE CONTROL

You may get wet or you may have a rough ride, but at least by opening the throttle you are greatly reducing the chances of the boat capsizing which is a far more serious problem to contend with. With an inflatable boat, the throttle is the most important control that you have. Open the throttle and not only does the boat power forward but you will also notice that there is a change of trim with the bow lifting. Close the throttle and the bow will drop. As we have already seen, you can use this change of trim to help drive the boat through waves. In a head sea the temptation is to close the throttle as you approach a wave; this is the *wrong* thing to do because it will cause the bow to drop and the boat is not moving in sympathy with the approaching wave. If instead you open the throttle at this point, the boat may accelerate slightly, but much more importantly, the bow will lift and this will help the boat to negotiate the wave more easily. It only needs a quick burst on the throttle to get this lift. Nearing the crest, you close the throttle, then the bow will drop and the boat is in a better attitude to pass

An Atlantic 21 rigid inflatable rescue boat operating in difficult sea conditions. *Photo: Peter Hadfield/RNLI*

through the crest and drop down the other side, when of course you open the throttle to cope with the next wave. These constant throttle adjustments do require concentration but you will make progress a lot more comfortably in head seas and after some practice you will learn to read the waves.

In a beam sea the object is to accelerate or decelerate to take advantage of the areas of flatter water and to avoid any breaking crests which may loom up to windward. One of the joys of driving an inflatable is its tremendous responsiveness, and whilst you need one hand for steering when you have remote controls, the other hand should be constantly on the throttle adjusting the speed and the trim to match the conditions. With smaller inflatables, the tiller steering on the less powerful engines is a tremendous advantage when operating in waves. With this type of control it is a one-handed operation for both steering and throttle, which leaves you with the other hand to hold on with and steady yourself.

On inflatables it is rare to find a power trim system or flaps which allow you to adjust the trim of the boat in a more defined way. If you have these controls, then in a head sea you probably want the flaps down or the power trim trimmed out to prevent the bow lifting too much to approaching waves. In following seas it is the reverse and, as a rule, you want the bow to lift which means tucking the power trim in and keeping the flaps horizontal. Without these controls you have to rely on the throttle as your main trimming aid, but you can use your crew as movable ballast. Certainly when going out through surf or over a bar, you will want to have the crew move as far forward as possible to keep the bow down just as the boat lifts to the wave, and move aft once the boat has gone through the crest. In a following sea they should move aft to concentrate their

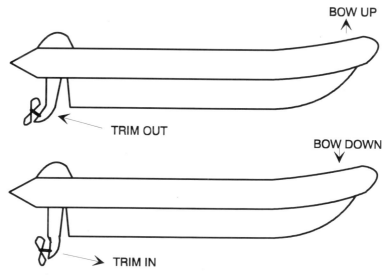

How power trim works. When the engine is trimmed in the bow is kept down, which is best for head sea operation. The engine is trimmed out both to produce maximum speed and when driving in a following sea, where it helps to lift the bow.

weight in this area. It requires team work and concentration for the crewmen to use their weight to the best advantage. This is the theory, but carrying it out in practice is less easy; in breaking waves, the crewman will have his work cut out just hanging on!

RIDING THE WAVES

It is important, in all sea conditions for the helmsman to have regard for his crew. The helmsman can anticipate what is happening up ahead and is concentrating on the waves, and he is in control. This means that he can assess the reactions of the boat and brace himself or hang on as necessary. The crewmen are less able to anticipate what is going to happen and relaxing their grip on the handholds could see them flying over the side if the motion is violent or unexpected. This can be a very real risk with the bounciness of an inflatable, and a responsible helmsman should give his crew as comfortable a ride as possible.

Another factor which can be used to improve the ride of inflatables is pressure adjustment of the air tubes. The tendency is to pump up inflatables as hard as reasonably possible in order to keep their shape because the air tube contributes to the longitudinal rigidity of the boat. However, bear in mind that when the tubes are pumped up hard and hit a wave there is very little 'give'; the boat will spring up and away from the water and cause a very bouncy and uncomfortable ride. By reducing the overall pressure in the tubes, perhaps with the forward compartments being at a lower pressure than the rear compartments, the air tubes will be able to absorb the shock of impact much better. This doesn't mean that you should make the tubes soft and flabby, but simply reduce them from the drum tight state in which they are normally kept. If you have launched the boat from the shore, then to a certain extent this will happen anyway. Simply putting the boat into cold water will reduce the temperature of the air inside the tubes and this in turn will reduce the pressure. If you do adopt this tactic then you need to be careful not to reduce the pressure too much or the longitudinal stiffness of the boat will be lessened which could put extra strain on the rigid floors and cause them to crack or break.

HARBOUR MANOEUVRES

When entering harbour in an inflatable, the basic skills are similar to those required for other boat handling, although with a built-in fender you can usually get away with unskilful boat handling without any consequential damage or hurt to your pride. However, if you want to do things properly and try and make a good job of coming alongside or berthing the boat, there are two important factors to bear in mind. One is that when you close the throttle, and take the engine out of gear, the boat will stop almost instantaneously and will not carry way like a conventional boat. In this situation, an inflatable will be rapidly affected by the wind rather than by the tide. The trick here is to maintain steering control by keeping power on, at least at idling speeds, right up until the minute you are virtually alongside.

As we already know, an inflatable has a tendency to skate sideways over the water. The boat has virtually no grip on the water and there is very little for the steering thrust to react against. When you steer sideways it actually makes the boat skid sideways as well as turning it. Practice will give you the skills for handling an inflatable in harbour, and if you can find a deserted jetty, or perhaps a larger vessel anchored at a mooring, then this could provide you with a good practice area. Try manoeuvring in winds of different directions and strengths, and with and without tides. The aim should be to come alongside gently and under control; because an inflatable will invariably bounce, however carefully you come alongside, have a line ready to tie up the boat, or at least be ready to grab the jetty to prevent the boat bouncing off so making you go through the whole manoeuvre again.

ANCHORING
The technique of anchoring an inflatable is similar to that used for any other craft except of course that the anchor line has to pass over the inflatable tube. You may want to anchor to go for a swim or for fishing, or of course you may want to use the anchor in an emergency if the engine has broken down. The anchoring process itself is straightforward; you simply throw the anchor over, pay out enough line to give at least three or four times the depth of the water, and then wait till the boat backs off downwind or tide, and the anchor line comes tight. However, if you plan to anchor for any length of time, then you will need to protect the inflatable tube from chafe at the point where the anchor line runs over it. You can do this quite easily by wrapping a piece of rag around the line. To prevent the boat sheering about when at anchor, it is best to make the anchor line fast as far forward as possible, and the bow ring is the best place if you can reach it. Tying off the anchor line here also gets rid of the chafe problem on the air tube. Another solution is to pass the anchor line through the bow ring and then bring it back on board which effectively means that you are anchored from the bow ring. This solution will stop the boat swinging and, perhaps more importantly, will stop the anchor line moving around over the air tube and being a potential cause of trouble. (See also page 63–5.)

Handling rigid inflatables (RIBs)

Much of what has been said about handling inflatable boats will also apply to RIBs. However, the significant difference between an inflatable and a RIB is the shape of the bottom of the boat; the rigid inflatable having a deep vee hull, whereas the inflatable is almost flat. The deep vee bottom and deeper draft gives a much better grip on the water so the RIB will be less affected by the wind. However, when launching off an open beach or when trailer-launching you will need to go in to deeper water before the engine can be lowered and started. Rigid inflatables generally have long shaft outboards and instead of the half-metre depth that you might require for an inflatable, this can increase to close to a metre with a RIB. If you add to this the extra weight of the hull, then it can become quite a handful for beach launching; larger sizes of rigid inflatable tend to be harbour based craft.

When handling a RIB in harbour for coming alongside or when going alongside another craft, then it handles very much like a conventional hard hulled boat. It will carry way in a more predictable manner when the engine is in neutral, so that you can use conventional boat handling techniques in harbour: approaching a jetty or another craft at a shallow angle and then swinging the stern in and cutting the engine as you come alongside. With the rigid inflatable, you can use the tide very effectively to help you come alongside.

COMING ALONGSIDE LARGE VESSELS

Many rigid inflatables, used professionally, operate from mother ships and there are well established techniques for coming alongside in open sea conditions. When the mother ship has headway there is a very defined flow of water from the bow which will tend to push the RIB off if it gets caught in this flow. Rather than taking up station a few boat lengths away from the ship and then trying to ease in towards the point where you want to land alongside, the best approach is from a point 30 or 40° on the quarter. This approach should keep you inside the water flow from off the bow and enable you to drive virtually straight to the landing point alongside. Ships at varying speeds will have different flow patterns coming off the hull; it can pay, therefore, to watch the pattern of waves before coming alongside a strange vessel. In general, the best point for landing alongside the hull is just aft of amidships but it is best to study the conditions before making up your mind. Often, there will be little choice simply because the boarding point on that ship cannot be moved. When operating in the open

Coming alongside a ship at sea. Rigid inflatables are now widely used from mother ships in the offshore oil industry, by navies, and on patrol and protection duties.

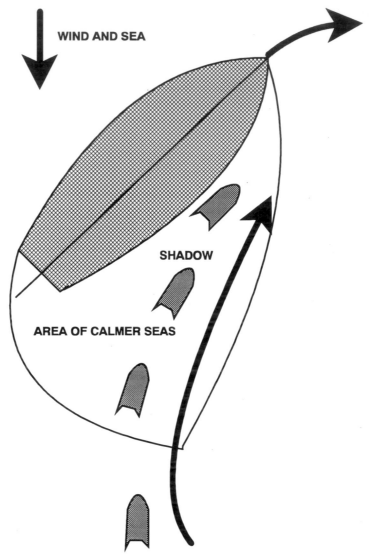

WIND AND SEA

SHADOW

AREA OF CALMER SEAS

Coming alongside a ship at sea. If the ship swings away from the wind and sea, it creates a temporary lee which can give almost calm conditions alongside for a transfer or for boat recovery.

sea alongside a ship, a lee should be created for the approaching boat. The best way for the ship to do this is to head first into the wind and sea, then swing towards the side the boat will come alongside. This will create a calm area of water under the lee of the hull and if a heading of 30 to 40° is maintained off the wind this should create the best conditions alongside. If the aim is to make a quick transfer of personnel or stores, then it is possible to hold the boat alongside simply by using the engine and steering. The bow of the RIB will be pinned lightly alongside the ship provided it maintains slow headway to create a flow of water along the hull.

Alternatively, if you need to tie up alongside, then take a painter from the mother ship; a long line led well forward will let the boat lie more comfortably alongside. With such a line it is possible to sheer off a little bit from the mother ship so that you are not constantly banging alongside.

DRIVING ON THE OPEN SEA

When driving a rigid inflatable in open sea conditions you will find that it has a much more positive feel than an inflatable. The tapering sides of the deep vee hull act as a cushion when the boat moves through the waves; this means that the boat is less sensitive to every slight change in shape of the wave. You can power more readily through waves with a predictable motion, which the crew will certainly find more acceptable. The variable geometry of the air tubes, as they hit the waves combined with the deep vee hull allow the rigid inflatable to be driven very hard at sea. It makes a great show when the boat flies out of the water in great clouds of spray. This may look impressive, but, in fact, it puts a very heavy strain on the crew, the boat and the engine. With a RIB, the secret of successful driving is to try to keep the boat firmly glued to the water. It may occasionally fly off the crest of a wave, but even when it does so it should still be under control. You have to appreciate that once a boat is airborne control is lost. Whilst mostly it will land predictably and relatively comfortably, that loss of control is not conducive to good driving. Equally, you are unlikely to make faster progress by using excessive throttle than if you try and keep the driving controlled, because when you lose control of the boat you come to a virtual standstill and then you have to pick up speed again. It is much better to make controlled progress which may not look so spectacular but is much kinder to the boat, the crew and the equipment. Controlled driving is done largely by using the throttle sympathetically. You open and close the throttle using the same driving technique as you do with an inflatable, easing the boat over wave crests rather than powering it blindly through them. On a large rigid inflatable you may have power trim available, in which case the drive is trimmed out in calmer waters to give more efficient propulsion but trimmed in when operating in rough conditions to keep the bow up. This will certainly be the case in a following sea, but in a head sea it can pay to trim the drive out a little to help keep the bow down. However, the throttle is still the most important control and it will give you a much more instantaneous and responsive trim control as well as controlling the speed at which you attack the waves. (See also page 83.)

Rigid inflatables tend to have seated driving positions with a conventional wheel and single lever throttle. This means that both hands are fully occupied when driving the boat and you do need a good seating position where you can securely locate yourself, otherwise the steering wheel tends to be used more as a handhold than for steering. As we saw in Chapter 5, to give effective control, the throttle lever also needs to be well positioned for ease of operation and for instantaneous reactions; ideally there should be some form of arm rest so that you can have positive throttle control.

Powering through waves in a following sea makes it especially important to have a suitable self-draining system so that water can exit rapidly. If you bury the bow into the wave in front, much of the resulting great fan of spray will come down on to the boat. This brings us to one of the biggest problems found when handling a rigid inflatable: the boat is so forgiving, no matter how you drive it, that you build up a feeling that you are invulnerable to whatever the sea can throw at you. Rigid inflatables do tend to be driven much harder than conventional craft, often close to the limits. One of the safety factors with a RIB is that the crew are likely to give in before the boat does, which means that you will probably frighten yourself before you do serious damage to the boat. One area where the rigid inflatable is vulnerable, and this has to be constantly borne in mind is that there is a risk of capsize if the boat is driven slower than the wave speed in following seas. This is the Achilles heel of the rigid inflatable and if a capsize does occur it is likely to be very sudden, so that one minute you are going along quite happily and the next minute you are upside down.

CAPSIZING A RIB

With RIBs and inflatables the risk of capsizing tends to occur when you are going slowly in following seas. You are most vulnerable when you are being cautious in landing on beaches and going through surf, or when passing through breaking waves on a harbour bar, with the wind and sea astern. You may be inclined to throttle back to see what is happening ahead when you should be much more concerned with what is going on behind you. It can be quite frightening to look around and see a big curling crest catching up with you and rising up over the stern because you have slowed down. You then have to act fast, rather than staring in fascination at the approaching wave, wind the throttle wide open and power away from it. Even if it does catch you as it breaks, if you have full power on you will also have full steering control and the chances are that you will be able to prevent the boat from being knocked sideways and rolled over in a capsize.

If you are operating in a beam sea, you may suddenly find a big wave rearing as a vertical wall of water alongside you. It can happen if you lose concentration for a moment, but once again the remedy is simple. Open the throttle, point the boat slightly down wind and power yourself out of trouble. This technique of opening the throttle to get yourself out of trouble is worth practicing under controlled conditions if you can. As a general rule, both with inflatables and RIBs, if you feel you are getting into trouble, the solution is to open the throttle and drive away from the problem. This broad generalisation will cope with most immediate problems but shouldn't be used as a substitute for careless or relaxed driving. The biggest requirement when driving inflatables or RIBs is concentration and you are really only likely to get caught out, even in quite severe conditions, if you are inattentive.

At night-time, driving any small fast boat is hazardous. The main problem is that you cannot read the waves and so you will have to be a lot more alert and cautious, only driving the boat well within its limits. There is no real solution to the night driving problem except intense concentration but try always to keep something in hand for the unexpected. In your favour will be the very quick responses of the controls which should help to keep you out of trouble. If you find a throttle setting which gives the boat a comfortable ride in most conditions you will have something in reserve when a larger than normal wave comes along.

Water jets

In winding up this chapter on boat handling, it is worth mentioning the techniques for use with water jet propulsion which is now widely used on many professional rigid inflatables. The water jet replaces the propellers which are vulnerable when operating in shallow water such as beaches, or harbour bars; it is also a much safer propulsion system for rescue boats which may have to retrieve casualties from the water. Out in the open sea, the techniques of driving with a water jet are very similar to those using a propeller. Here the throttle is still the main control, and you will get the change of trim associated with opening or closing it. With some water jets you can get a loss of thrust when the jet picks up aerated water. The onset of this might be faster than the similar effect you get from propellers, simply because the water jet intake is less deeply immersed than a propeller. However in general this can be a safety feature, because in this type of aerated water, you should probably be slowing down rather than speeding up, and the loss of thrust is only likely to be very temporary. Unlike a cavitating propeller where you have to close the throttle to allow it to get a grip again, the water jet will pick up power automatically as soon as it hits solid water and you don't have to close the throttle before getting thrust.

It is when you are manoeuvring in harbour that most helmsmen find difficulties with a water jet. You feel the need for three hands to cope with the controls on a water jet. There is the steering, which is incorporated into the water jet, the reverse and ahead bucket which has its own lever and then there is the throttle. This compares with the two-handed operation of the wheel and combined throttle/gear lever found with outboards or stern drives. The best technique to use when manoeuvring in harbour with a water jet is to set the throttle at a speed slightly above idling and then switch your concentration on to the bucket control which will give you the ahead and astern, and the neutral in between. With the bucket you have very delicate control of the thrust in both directions, and unlike an outboard, you also still retain full steering control even when the bucket is in the neutral position. The controls of a water jet do take some getting used to, particularly if you have been used to more conventional controls, but once you master this technique, you will find that you have far superior control in confined waters.

CHAPTER 7

NAVIGATION AND WEATHER

There are times when you are driving an inflatable or RIB when navigation is a sub-conscious art. You know where you are and you can see where you are going and you can steer a straight line between the two. It's a straight-forward exercise and you are barely conscious that you are navigating along the route you follow. However, behind this type of navigation lies the presumption that you know that there are no hidden dangers under the water along the chosen route and that visibility is not going to close down, so that you will always be able to see where you are going. Behind this presumption lies a degree of experience; perhaps you have been along the route before or you have previously studied the charts, and you have also listened to the weather forecast. All in all, you have a pretty fair idea of what is going on and what is going to happen, and behind this apparent casual approach to navigation lies a degree of pre-planning and experience.

This type of approach will be followed when going ashore from a yacht in a small inflatable. Here you will be following an obvious channel, or even if you are not aware of one you will not be too concerned about the conse-quences of going astray because you are travelling at a very slow speed and the prospects of damage or injury are extremely slight. You may suffer a hurt to your pride if you go aground, but the chances are that no one is going to notice and you will come off as quickly as you went aground.

Where your navigation starts to get stretched is when you are running on a coastal passage or driving out to a diving location. You may run into fog or rough seas, giving poor visibility and under these conditions, you will be concentrating more on driving the boat than on navigation. Another case can be when you are going out on a search and rescue oper-ation or when operating outside sighting range of land or at night time. These, and many more situations, will start to require a more serious approach to navigation if you aim to get where you are going with a reasonable degree of certainty.

Pilotage

There are two main approaches to navigation in inflatables and RIBs. One is what might be termed 'eyeball navigation' or pilotage which involves using a chart and the most basic of instruments such as a compass and a watch. With this type of navigation, experience can be vital in order to get things right. The alternative is to use electronic navigation, and now that sophisticated electronics can cope with the harsh environment of the inflatable or RIB, electronics have now become a viable means of navigation and one which takes a lot of the guesswork out of the situation and enables you to be much more precise and accurate.

With both types of navigation, a degree of pre-planning is essential. You don't have a chart table on board the boat and even spreading out a chart and using it is virtually impossible unless you stop the boat to work things out. It is much better to study the chart beforehand in a comfortable environment on shore where you can get out your parallel rules and dividers and draw the courses and measure the distances and positions to where you want to go. Once you have drawn the lines on the chart, then check them very carefully to make sure that there are no underwater dangers close to your proposed route. Anything within half a mile of the route should be considered a potential danger and given a wide berth because if you are doing eyeball navigation you have no guarantee that you can navigate to any higher degree of accuracy. Once you have checked out the course you have drawn on the chart then, if you are using electronic navigation, you measure the latitude and longitude of every point where the course is altered, and these can be transferred into the electronic navigation equipment as waypoints. We will look at this electronic navigation later, but here we are concerned with eyeball navigation. Here the latitude and longitude are no use to you because you have no means of establishing them. What you have to do is check your position by other means which will usually entail visual sightings; from these sightings you can get an idea of where you are and perhaps more importantly, where you are going.

Because you are relying on visual sightings you need to make best use of what is available along or close to your chosen route. Check out the course that you are proposing to follow and see if there are any buoys or beacons within a mile or so of the course line. Passing close to a buoy or beacon gives you a very precise position fix as it is marked on the chart. It can often pay you to alter your direct course between two points in order to pass close to a buoy or beacon even if this means travelling for a slightly longer distance. This position check along your route will be extremely valuable and will make you feel a lot more comfortable about your navigation.

Buoy hopping can be an extremely good way of navigating in inflatables and you can use the same technique when running along a coastline where you go from headland to headland. If you set a direct course in a straight line with no checks from start to finish along the route, you could find yourself some way off course when you approach your destination, with the consequent anxiety and risk that this uncertainty can bring. A good technique is to plan the route to give the shortest possible distances or legs between points where you can fix your position by visual observation, generally by passing close to the buoy or headland or any other distinctive feature.

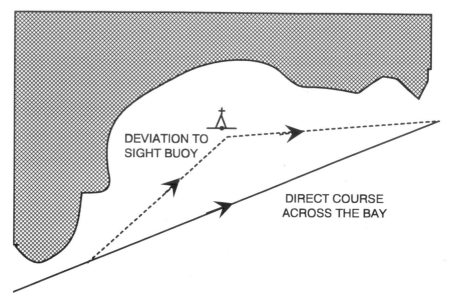

Navigation along a coastline. It can be better to divert into the bay where there is a mark rather than to take the direct route across the bay between headlands. This shortens the distance you have to steer on a compass course.

There are many other clues which can be gleaned from the chart to check your course and position as you go along. Try extending a course line beyond the point where you alter course and see if it crosses the land or passes close to a distinctive feature. Perhaps there will be a conspicuous building marked on the chart close to where this extension of the course line meets the coast. This means that you can use this charted feature for steering direction rather than trying to watch a compass and it will also give you confirmation that you are on the correct route. Even more positive, is a transit bearing when you have two fixed points in line. This could be a beacon and the headland behind it on the shore, or other fixed features which you can identify from the chart. When these two points are in line you must lie somewhere along the line which extends outward from those points; this is called the transit bearing. This will not give you a precise position but at least a reasonable indication of where you are.

Shallow water can often give you a clue about your position and whilst you may not be able to see the shallows you may well be able to see waves which are breaking in the vicinity. This can give you a clue about where the shallow water lies and if you know where it is from the chart, it is comparatively easy to steer a course to keep clear. Rocks can also be used to give you a clue about your location and even wrecks can serve their purpose as a warning if they show above water and are marked on the chart. Study the chart carefully because it is a mine of information, not only about what is going on that you can see, but also what is going on *under* the water. The chart is your bible when you are navigating and it is surprising just how much information it contains.

If you have been out of sight of land there are techniques you can adopt to make the landfall more positive. If you aim directly for the headland then all will be well if you make a reasonably precise landfall and everything goes according to plan. However the chances are that you will be one side or the other of the course line which should not pose any problem provided that your landfall is inside the headland. However if it is outside the headland and the visibility is poor, then you could go past and miss it altogether, and not realise what is going on.

The aim with all navigation is to try and remove the uncertainty. The solution in this case is to make sure that your landfall will be inside the headland by creating a bias in the course. If you aim for a point which is two or three miles inside the headland then you have a good safety margin and will sight land even if you are some way off course. Once you sight land then you can steer up for the headland. Check on the chart that there are no off-lying rocks or dangers inside the headland which could pose a hazard to making a landfall in poor visibility. The main advantage of adopting this technique is that you know which way to turn to find the headland when you do sight land. You can use a similar technique when making a landfall on a low and fairly featureless coast. Perhaps you are aiming for a harbour which is not likely to show up well against the background hills from a distance. The solution here is to aim to make your landfall two or three miles one side or the other of the harbour entrance and that way when you sight the land and don't see the harbour right ahead, at least you will know which way to turn to find the harbour entrance. If you aim directly for the harbour entrance and then you don't see it ahead you have only a 50% chance of turning the right way in order to find the entrance. These are the sort of techniques you can develop to make your navigation more positive and more precise and take some of the guesswork out of the situation.

In a rigid inflatable, you have to bear in mind that steering a compass course over a considerable distance, perhaps 20 miles or more, could lead to quite large errors. The compass is rarely still in the RIB and you have to try and mentally average it out. Trying to steer a reasonably precise course is difficult and both wind and tide can affect the course that you make good over the ground. It is very difficult to make precise corrections for the wind effect, if it is on the beam, for you have to estimate what the affect will be. Normally you will add 5, 10 or 20 degrees to the course to counteract the wind effect; only experience can tell you how much to allow. With tides you can be a bit more precise by looking at the tidal atlas and working out how much effect the tide will have on the course that you make. But the effect of the tide will be related to speed made good and you don't always know that until you are out at sea. At the end of the day, you will have to bear in mind that if you manage to steer any required course within 10 degrees, then you are probably doing very well and you must make allowances for this type of error to occur when planning your landfall. So, we see that a bit of pre-planning by building a bias into the course and making the legs as short as possible will take a great deal of the guesswork out of the landfall, particularly in poor visibility. In addition to giving you self-confidence in your navigation ability it will also convince your crew that you know what you are doing!

DIVERSIONS INTO BAYS

If you are planning a route along a coastline, the logical course is going to be to travel from headland to headland, ignoring the areas of water inside the bay. However, if you adopt this approach you are not always going to make the best and most comfortable progress and if the bays are wide then you will have the worry of trying to make a landfall at each headland. One solution here can be to set a course inside the bay, not necessarily right round the edge of it but at least a positive diversion into the bay, so that firstly you can keep sight of the land and keep a check on your position, secondly you can often keep out of the stronger parts of the tide (well worthwhile if the wind is against the tide) and thirdly you can often get shelter from the land if the wind is offshore. The longer distance can often be justified through one or more of these benefits, always assuming that you have enough fuel to cover the extra distance.

This diversion into the bay can be of great benefit in lively sea conditions. Particularly when the wind is directly ahead on a course from headland to headland, diverting into the bay can give you a more comfortable ride because the wind is then 30 or 40 degrees on the bow rather than dead ahead. This has the effect of making the wave lengths longer which effectively reduces their gradient. It also means that as you get into the bay,

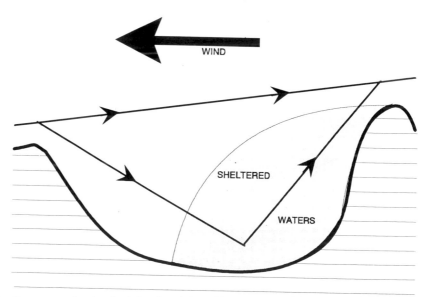

Another reason for steering into a bay is to get better sea conditions. The direct route is fully exposed to a head wind and sea, whilst the longer route into the bay puts the wind on the bow in the early stages and allows you to take advantage of the better conditions inshore. This inshore route also makes navigation easier, but it can increase fuel consumption.

you are steadily getting the benefit of the shelter of the approaching head-land, so you will be driving into calmer waters all the time helping you to make better speed although you will have to turn back into the rougher conditions in order to round the next headland.

With the shallow draft and excellent manoeuvrability of an inflatable or RIB, your technique for rounding headlands can also take advantage of any smoother conditions which often appear close in. Where there are strong tidal streams you will often find a relatively calm patch off a head-land, perhaps only 200 or 300 metres wide, close inshore. Further out from the headland there are often tidal races which can be particularly danger-ous to small boats. By taking inshore passages you can save a great deal of time and effort, but once again you will need to do some homework on the chart to take maximum advantage of the situation. The ideal situation is where there is relatively deep water and no off-lying dangers extending out from the headland, which means that you can pass round close to, hopefully finding better conditions in this area where the tides are weak or non-existent. Even when there are rocks or shallows there it is often possible to find a way through because of the very shallow draft of an inflatable or RIB. Providing there is a degree of lift in the water from the swell, any dangers will show as broken water and if you keep a careful watch you will be able to see the dangers long before you hit them. Even in poor visibility, you can adopt this technique provided that you have done your homework on the chart and are confident that there is a way through. Take it easy and go through at low speed so that even if you see something you don't like very close ahead, there is still time to stop or alter course.

TIDE CHECKS
Although the speed of most inflatables or RIBs makes the strength of the tidal streams less of a problem for navigation, part of your pre-planning routine should be to check what the tide will be doing at different places along the route, in terms of its strength and direction and height. Indeed, the height of the tide at different times may be more important than the strength and direction because this will often determine what inshore channels are viable. Just as important, it will determine what rocks and shoals will be visible and which will be covered towards high water. Your pre-planning in this respect should not only include knowing what is going on along your intended course, but also in adjacent waters in case you plan to divert, or the conditions become more difficult and you want to shorten the trip and go inshore. You should also check which harbours are available in case you have engine trouble or other problems, or in case you need to seek shelter. Bear in mind that if conditions do deteriorate, a harbour downwind may provide you with a relatively easy trip in the pre-vailing sea conditions but the entrance itself could be dangerous because of the onshore wind; these conditions would be made even worse if an ebb tide is running out of the harbour and there is shallow water.

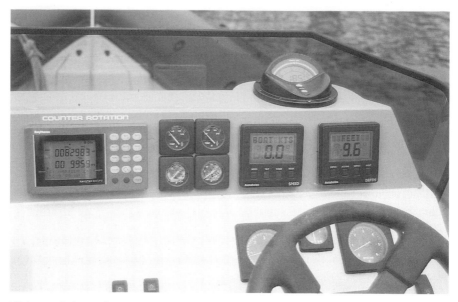

Waterproof electronics mounted in a console now enable inflatables and RIBs to get the full benefits of modern navigation methods.

Electronic navigation equipment

Navigation with electronic aids can take a great deal of the guesswork out of the situation and when everything is working it all looks so simple, but it is very easy to get lulled into a false sense of security. By all means use an electronic position finder as your primary means of navigation but don't let it stop you from doing your homework before you set out and checking on all the options which are open to you. Electronic equipment may be working close to its survivability limits in an inflatable or RIB, and you cannot trust it 100% to keep working. Even though the electronics may survive, there is always the risk that the electrical system which supplies it may pack up, so you should always be prepared for this. At least have a mental picture of the navigation situation, and some idea of the courses and distances involved so that you can find your way to your destination or at least to safety without the electronic position finder. It really is just a simple matter of going back to the eyeball navigation techniques mentioned earlier. If these are going to work successfully then you need to have done the same sort of planning beforehand. There are various aspects to electronic navigation and the first we will look at here is the choice of electronic equipment.

WHICH ELECTRONIC SYSTEM DO YOU CHOOSE?
Fixing your position by electronic means is the basis of electronic navigation, and here there are three choices available.

Loran C, is available for position fixing in the USA and in some parts of

Europe. Loran C is a system where transmissions are sent out from land-based transmitters in a special sequence and a receiver on board measures the time of reception of transmissions from different shore stations; from this it is possible to calculate the position. The accuracy is generally adequate for inflatable boat navigation, in good areas it is about 20 metres but in areas of poor coverage it may be 200 or 300 metres out. Overall it is more than adequate for most requirements. However it does suffer from the disadvantage that the errors can effectively double at certain times of the day, particularly at dawn and dusk and the transmissions can be affected by electrical storms and to a certain extent by land features. However despite these drawbacks, Loran C certainly remains a viable navigation system and expansion of the system in Europe should lead to complete coverage over the whole of northern Europe to supplement the existing coverage in the Mediterranean area. The big advantage of Loran C is that the receivers are the cheapest available on the market. Waterproof receivers are widely available, and you can also get receivers which incorporate other features such as plotters.

Decca Navigator is a similar system but it has a shorter effective range from the transmitters and its coverage is limited to the British Isles and much of the waters of northern Europe. In terms of accuracy there is little to choose between Decca Navigator and Loran C and there is not a lot of difference in the price of the receivers. However, as the market is more limited for Decca, the production quantities tend to be smaller and therefore the price has not reduced to the same extent as has happened with Loran C. The main difference between the two systems is that Decca Navigator measures a phase difference between signals from different transmitters as opposed to the time difference measured with Loran C, but the accuracies are comparable. With Decca Navigator there are also areas where coverage is poor, particularly when very close to transmitters, and again at dawn and dusk and in electrical storms.

Global Positioning System (GPS) is the latest development in electronic navigation, and is set to supercede all the others both in terms of accuracy and reliability. GPS operates on transmissions from satellites rather than from terrestrial stations and effectively measures the time difference between the time a signal is transmitted until the time it is received from a series of satellites circling the earth. From these measurements it is possible to establish the range and with the range from three or four satellites it is then possible to fix a position very precisely. As you can imagine, with moving satellites the computations are very complex, but the modern computer can handle these quite easily, and even though the current transmissions are artificially degraded to reduce the accuracy for non-military users, the position is accurate to within 100 metres 95% of the time, which is more than adequate for inflatable navigation. GPS is certainly the way ahead in terms of electronic navigation but currently the price of the receivers is around twice those of Loran and Decca so often the user's choice depends, to a great deal, on how much he is prepared to invest. Obviously if money is no object then GPS is the way to go, but if funds are constrained, then Loran C or Decca Navigator can provide viable substitutes.

Whichever system is selected, the method of navigation is much the same. You plot your route on the chart and then take off a latitude and longitude at each point where it is proposed to alter course. These *waypoints* are entered into the navigation receiver in the waypoint catalogue. They are

Navigation made easy with a windscreen chart display. It still allows the helmsman to look over the top of the screen.

each given a number and it is then a simple matter to programme the receiver to follow the route between consecutive waypoints. The receiver knows where it is all the time and is able to calculate the course and speed made good. This is useful, but much more importantly the GPS receiver can calculate the current position in relation to the next waypoint which enables it to tell you the course and distance to the next course alteration. Perhaps the most valuable information it provides is to tell you your *cross track error*. This is the distance you are one side or the other of the direct line between two waypoints; ie how far you are off course. Knowing this enables you to alter course to bring the boat back on to the correct track and course for the next waypoint. This means that you have all the information necessary to follow a prescribed route with an accuracy of about 100 metres, simply by looking at the numbers on the navigation receiver display.

Most of the time you can rely on the receiver numbers to be accurate but navigators are much more familiar with a graphic display such as seen on the paper chart. Because of this, many navigation receiver manufacturers have introduced a plotting mode into the display. This shows graphically where you are in relation to where you want to be and it is much easier to picture what is going on than from the numbers. A graphic display will show the direct line from one waypoint to the next and also the actual track that you are following plotted in real time. Missing from this graphic display are the shoals and land features which would be seen on the paper chart. However electronic chart systems are obtainable which use a larger type of screen and show a section of the chart and plot the vessel moving across it. This is the ultimate in navigation sophistication; with such a display you have virtually all the information you need at your fingertips because not only can you see where you are, where you are going and where you want to be, but also the dangers and features which are around you. These electronic chart displays are now available in waterproof form using a flat screen which takes up the minimum of space. They will work in the inflatable environment but at present they are expensive and would really only be justified in an inflatable or RIB for professional use which had to undertake serious navigation tasks.

Hand-held GPS receivers, which are battery powered and waterproof, are ideal for use on inflatables. These receivers are almost pocket-sized and are self-contained units. Whilst the battery life may be only a few hours, these receivers can provide a good backup to visual navigation; you can just switch on when you are unsure about your position so that you can get home safely if conditions deteriorate. They also have the added advantage that there is no need for fixed installation and the receivers can be taken home for security.

ECHO SOUNDERS AND RADAR

Depth measurement can also be done electronically. An echo sounder can be very useful, particularly if you are navigating close inshore or in shallow waters. It won't tell you what is going on ahead of you but at least

A rigid inflatable rescue boat in New Zealand showing the type of complex superstructure which can be fitted to these boats. *Photo: Naiad.*

it will give you some sort of warning if the depths start to shoal. Fitting an echo sounder into a RIB is fairly easy because of the hard hull, but on an inflatable boat the transducer has to be mounted on the transom. Echo sounders, particularly those of the more sophisticated type with a contour display can be very useful for divers who want to locate wrecks which can be seen in profile on the sea bed.

It is even possible to fit radar on to a large rigid inflatable. Any boat over 7 metres in length could accommodate a radar set, but the main problem is to find a secure mounting for the antenna which, even on the smallest unit, is 0.7 metres in diameter. This can be mounted on a roll bar, and with modern sets now being available with flat screens and in water-tight form, it is possible to mount the display in the open so that the unit can be used effectively. Radar can be a very good method of checking the navigation results produced by an electronic position fixing receiver. It does require a degree of experience to interpret the picture on the radar, as it is never quite as precise as that shown on the electronic chart. This is because you have to visualise the view point of the radar, which is a hori-zontal view taken from the antenna looking outward. This has to be matched against the plan view of the display, so that some of the features which you might expect to see on the display are not always visible because they are hidden one behind the other. You can also get problems with the wide beam angle produced by the very small antenna which would be used on a rigid inflatable. This wide beam angle, which can be up to 5 degrees, could encompass anything within that 5 degree sector as a single target at a certain range, which means that a narrow harbour entrance would not show up as an entrance until you were quite close to it, or two buoys close together could show up as one. The important thing with radar is experience, and you need to use the radar quite a lot in order to get familiar with the way it presents information, and the weaknesses and strengths of the displayed information.

The ultimate in navigation systems for a rigid inflatable would be to have a waterproof radar and a waterproof electronic chart alongside each other. Simply by comparing the two displays you would have a very good picture of the whole navigation situation, and these displays both generate their information in real time. It is perhaps unrealistic to think that you could get the same navigation facility in an inflatable boat, partly because of the difficulty in finding somewhere to mount the equipment, and partly the problem of an adequate power supply. Also the environment of an inflatable boat is far less conducive to a good electronic equipment installation than is the case with a rigid inflatable.

The important consideration as far as electronic navigation is concerned, is to make sure that the equipment is effectively installed. There is nothing worse than unreliable electronics and reliability can only be achieved by very careful attention to every detail of the installation. It goes without saying that all equipment should be waterproof and nothing less than *fully* watertight equipment should be considered. This applies to the connections going into the equipment at the back and all connections throughout both the electrical supply and the antennae. The electrical supply needs to be engineered with great care because it is often the source of weakness in electronic installations.

There is not usually much problem with interference when using a GPS or a radar installation, although the antennae for these two items of equipment should be kept as far apart as possible. With Loran C or Decca Navigator, the antennae should be installed as far away as possible from outboard engines because these tend to generate a lot of interference. Some of the electrical systems such as the alternator on a diesel engine boat can generate interference and so before making a permanent installation, test the interference levels with the engine running and the antenna mounted in a variety of positions before selecting the optimum one. Alternatively, you can line the hood of an outboard engine with a special metallic paint which effectively cuts down the electrical radiation from the engine.

Weather forecasts

The use of electronic navigation on inflatables and particularly on RIBs opens up a whole new dimension, enabling these boats to operate more effectively and undertake longer voyages. Modern boats can operate as independent units a long way offshore if necessary, given the right circumstances and operation, and electronic navigation has been another step in opening up more adventurous applications. However, this also makes weather conditions a much more important factor, and it is essential for inflatable and RIB operators to have an understanding of weather conditions and the potential for change. Weather forecasts should always be obtained before going to sea, but the important thing with forecasts is to remember that they are always couched in general rather than specific terms. A forecast may suggest that winds will increase to force 6 which may come close to the operating limit of a rigid inflatable, but if you have something important to do, you will want to know if that force 6 is going to arrive at 1400 or 1800 hours, and generally the forecast gives you very little help in this matter. By all means listen to the forecast and abide by what it says, as it is better to take the cautious route to recreational boating. You will probably miss some excellent days simply because the timing of the forecast was wrong rather than the forecast itself but you should always play it safe. For professional users, the forecast is even more important. When days represent income, then you want to know much more precisely what the weather is going to do. Here you have two options, one is to get your own personalised forecast from a meteorological office which can cost a considerable amount of money, or the other one is to get the weather charts and work out much more precisely what is happening exactly in the region where you plan to operate.

FRONTAL SYSTEMS
In order to analyse weather charts you need to have an understanding of weather fronts, how they occur and the type of weather that you can expect during their passage. It is perhaps outside the scope of this book to go into this detail, but suffice to say that if you get two weather charts which are 24 hours apart in terms of timing, you can then plot the progress of the weather fronts during this period, and interpellate for the particular time or position that interests you; then you can work out just when the front is likely to pass through your area. As most major changes of wind strength and direction are related to weather fronts, then this should give you a much better idea of what is going on with the weather and when and how you can expect changes to occur.

Many of the changes in the weather due to frontal systems will also be indicated by the clouds around you. Understanding changes in cloud formation will not only give you a forewarning of what is going on, but will also give you a much closer timing on the possibilities of change especially if you use these in conjunction with forecasts and forecast charts.

Whilst navigation may have moved away from the 'by guess and by God era', into a much more precise electronic age for weather and sea information, personal observation of what is going on around you is still vital to understand and anticipate the changes. Electronics can do a great deal in helping to tell you what is going on with the weather, but at the end of the day it is your own personal analysis and observation which completes the picture.

Radio communication

It is essential to be able to keep in touch with the outside world in an inflatable or a rigid inflatable. Communications can be vital to many operations such as search and rescue and police duties, but for the leisure user or the diver or the fisherman, they can provide vital updates for weather information and navigation warnings. The VHF radio operating on the marine band is the standard unit fitted to most RIBs these days whilst inflatable boats tend to rely on the hand-held units simply because of the difficulties of permanent installation. Installing a VHF radio needs the same attention to detail as required for electronic navigation equipment. Because the antenna is also for transmitting, you need to try and locate it at least a metre away from any of the receiving antennae for the electronic navigation equipment. Again, a waterproof radio is ideal for the inflatable or RIB environment and nothing less should be considered to be satisfactory if you want to operate it easily and efficiently. Waterproof loudspeakers are now available so that you can keep a listening watch on the radio, or alternatively, a head set is another possibility. One option is a waterproof headset with a boom microphone which allows you to operate the radio simply by pressing and releasing the transmit/receive button. This is the sort of equipment that many professionals might use, and in order to keep both hands free it is possible to have a foot operated transmit/receive switch, or even a voice activated unit.

CHAPTER 8

SAFETY AND SURVIVAL

It is very easy with the enthusiasm that comes from driving an inflatable, to forget about topics such as safety and survival. The inflatable is such a forgiving boat that you tend to get the feeling that it is invincible. The larger sizes of inflatable and RIB are among the most seaworthy boats ever produced and the problem is that they do tend to get driven near to, or at their limits. This means that when something does go wrong it tends to happen quite suddenly, and there is almost a feeling of surprise that the boat has let you down. You have to work quite hard to put a foot wrong with an inflatable, but you need to remember that *every* boat has its limits.

Safety comes from keeping within the operating parameters of a particular boat, and survival equates to being able to cope with the situation when you exceed these limits. There are two main considerations for safety and survival.

- **Personal survival:** protective clothing, lifejackets and similar items for survival in the marine environment.
- **Boat survival:** the action you take and the equipment to make sure that you can cope with most emergency situations.

Anticipation is the name of the game when it comes to safety and you should go through the 'what if' situation, trying to picture the sort of things which could go wrong and how you are likely to cope with them. You probably won't anticipate all the scenarios which can occur. The sea is notorious for throwing up situations which you wouldn't have dreamed could happen! In most emergencies it is the action that you take in the first few minutes which really counts and which dictates the outcome of the situation, and so the value of this anticipation cannot be overestimated.

Personal safety

It is important to appreciate on an inflatable or RIB that you are very exposed to the elements. You may be able to huddle behind a windscreen and get protection of a limited sort, or you may have the luxury of a small wheelhouse or dodger on larger craft, but mostly you have to accept that you are very exposed. On a hot, sunny day when you go to sea for fun it may be difficult to visualise the need for any protective clothing. The spray can have a nice cooling effect and the wind provides a comfortable breeze. However, if you return to base later in the evening, you could find the temperature dropping rapidly and the need for protection becomes obvious. Another potentially more serious situation is if something goes wrong: perhaps your engine breaks down and you are drifting at sea waiting for help and it turns cold. There can then be a serious risk of exposure so always take some sort of protective clothing to sea with you to guard against a change in the weather. Clothing is one of the easier items to stow away, and if you are lucky you will not have cause to use it, but if the conditions do change then having protective clothing on board will be worth its weight in gold.

There are four different categories of protective clothing which can be used in inflatables or RIBs:

- Thin lightweight waterproof jackets with a single skin will generally serve to keep you reasonably dry but perhaps more importantly provide a barrier against the wind.
- More substantial suits which generally have an inner lining and good seals at the ankles and wrists and perhaps even at the neck.
- Wet suits, much favoured by divers, which are made from foam neoprene rubber of varying thickness which provide an insulating barrier against the water but are not windproof when wet.
- Dry suits of neoprene or nylon membrane which usually incorporate boots and waterproof rubber seals at wrist and neck; they have a waterproof zip to allow entry and exit.

All of these categories of clothing have a role to play in inflatable boating. The selection is to a certain degree a personal choice, but it also depends on how you use the boat and the length of time that you tend to spend in the boat.

WATERPROOFS

Lightweight waterproofs are fine in summer when the conditions are warm and you go out perhaps for a swim or for fishing. You may find that you need to wear such clothing when the boat is travelling at speed and the wind chill factor starts to make its presence felt, but as soon as you stop you can take it off and relax in casual clothes. Lightweight protective clothing of this type should be on board at all times when the boat is being used and it will provide useful protection if you get caught out by changing conditions.

If you use your boat more seriously, extending its use outside summer days, then you will need something more than lightweight clothing. In colder conditions, the wind chill factor acting on rain or spray can produce very intense cooling. The lack of protection in the boat will accentuate this and without adequate clothing you will find yourself getting very cold, very quickly. Here you have a choice between the three more serious types of protective clothing, and each has its merits and its problems. Waterproof suits which usually consist of jacket and trousers, or can be one-piece garments have the benefit that they are easy to put on, comfortable to wear and can be worn over the top of normal clothing. Two-piece suits, made in modern materials with high waisted trousers, usually give good protection but the weak point is always around the neck where it is virtually impossible to get a positive seal. You have to rely on a towelling scarf to soak up the damp which percolates through. If you need to wear a suit for a long time, then a suit of this type is probably the most comfortable, and they are generally fitted with a hood which gives head protection. A great deal of body heat can be lost through the head and good protection here is vital in cold weather.

WET SUITS

The wet suit provides an insulating layer next to the body which remains effective no matter how wet you get, in fact they are more effective in the water than out of it. Out of water they are fine when dry, but if they get wet the evaporation of the water from the suit leads to a cooling effect. However, these suits are generally very adequate for use in inflatables and RIBs and when wearing one of these suits it really doesn't matter how wet you get. You do need to strip off all your clothes before getting into a wet

Here this pair of divers are well kitted up for cold water; head gear is essential to prevent heat loss. Even though conditions are calm, the cox is very sensibly wearing his lifejacket. *Photo: Carson Inflatables.*

suit and they do tend to have to be made to measure in order to give the tight fit. Wet suits come in a variety of shapes and forms but for serious inflatable boating the best one is a full one piece or two piece suit which incorporates a hood and is used with bootees to give overall protection. A close fitting wet suit can become uncomfortable during long periods and some people find that the material causes chafe around sensitive areas. For the diver the wet suit is ideal because it works equally well above (when combined with a wind-proof jacket) and below water, but if full weather protection is required then non-diving operators tend to prefer the dry suit.

DRY SUITS

The best dry suit for use on inflatables is that made from synthetic rubber-impregnated fabric rather similar to that used to make tubes for the boat, although obviously of a lighter grade. The soft rubber stretch seals at neck and wrists normally have to be cut to match the individual's size if the suit is to be worn comfortably over long periods. With the heavy duty boots incorporated into the suit, it is a very practical garment to wear for inflatable boating, keeping you bone dry inside so that they can be put on top of normal clothing. But because the suit is sealed and the fabric does not 'breathe' it can become rather hot and sweaty after a while.

HOODS, GOGGLES AND GLOVES

The dry suit doesn't have a hood built into it and the need for a hood, preferably of the lined type cannot be over-emphasised if you are operating a rigid inflatable in cold conditions. Some of the hoods found on normal protective clothing can cover both the mouth and the nose so that only the eyes are left exposed. A possible alternative, favoured by rescue boat crews, is to wear a crash helmet which provides protection from cold and impact. Head covering is essential in winter conditions to reduce the risks of exposure, and goggles, probably of the ski type, should also be worn to give eye protection. Goggles are invaluable on any boat which is travelling at over 30 knots as they save you from constantly rubbing your eyes to maintain vision. Hand protection can be just as vital. Probably the best type of gloves for use in an inflatable boat are those made from thin neoprene foam. These allow adequate finger movement and whilst this foam doesn't give the same protection as the thicker wet suit material, it certainly insulates the hand from the wind, and gives an acceptable level of protection.

SURVIVAL SUITS

If using an inflatable or RIB during cold winter months the crew need very effective protective clothing if they are to have a chance of both surviving and carrying out useful duties. When assessing clothing requirements you should always bear in mind that the wearer may end up being thrown overboard, and so the clothing may have to double up as an in-water survival suit. A recommended list of clothing for rigid inflatable crew members operating on North Sea oil industry rescue boats is as follows:

- Thermal undergarments
- A one piece fibre pile suit
- A dry suit with a front entry incorporating wrist seals and boots with toe protection
- Neoprene fingered mitts for hand protection
- A wool balaclava hood for head protection
- Ski goggles incorporating double lenses.

With this type of gear it is the first two items which provide the thermal insulation and the dry suit which provides the water seal to keep the water on the outside. The head protection could probably be improved by using a neoprene balaclava type helmet such as divers wear. This list gives you an idea of what is regarded professionally as an effective set of clothing which provides adequate thermal protection even if the wearer is in the water. It is important, however, that clothing does not restrict movement to the point where the wearer might find it difficult to operate the boat.

There are several types of survival suit on the market which aim to give the wearer a much longer period of survival even in ice-cold waters and for serious inflatable or RIB operators in the winter these might be considered as an alternative. However, many of these survival suits do not give the wearer particularly good mobility and so they are unsuitable for boat operators. There is a new type of survival suit coming on to the market which combines good protection for everyday wear as a normal working suit, but also incorporates a lifejacket which can be inflated when needed. Additionally, the suit itself can be inflated, creating a thermal layer which converts it almost instantly into a fully effective survival suit. Boots, hand mitts and head protection are incorporated, so these suits can be a very effective solution for the requirements of inflatable boat operators who operate in severe conditions. Such suits are expensive, and many users prefer the multi-layer approach to protection, such as that suggested for North Sea oil operators, so that the level of thermal insulation can be adjusted to suit the ambient conditions.

LIFEJACKETS
On the question of lifejackets, again there is also a choice. At one end of the range there is the SOLAS type of lifejacket, which uses fully inherent buoyancy usually of a comparatively hard closed-cell type of foam. These lifejackets are primarily designed for passenger ship use, and are not very suitable for use on inflatable boats. At the other end of the scale there is the compact inflatable lifejacket which is easily and unobtrusively worn over the top of protective clothing. It can be inflated either manually through an oral inflation tube, or by gas bottle simply by pulling on a lanyard. There are versions of this lifejacket which have automatic gas bottle inflation which inflates the lifejacket when you enter the water. In between

these two types there is a third type which has partial inherent buoyancy and partial air inflation buoyancy. With this choice of types of lifejacket you can select the level of protection which you feel appropriate for your personal requirements.

The main choice is whether you are prepared to risk having to inflate your lifejacket once you are in the water if you fall overboard. It is always argued that, if you see a risk situation developing, then with the inflatable type of lifejacket you can always put some air into the inflation chamber to provide some buoyancy. But with inflatables, emergencies tend to happen suddenly and the chance of recognising a developing situation and putting air into the lifejacket prior to an incident, is remote. So what you have to decide is whether the risk of going overboard unconscious can be balanced against the comfort of wearing a small unobtrusive lifejacket. The halfway house type of lifejacket with partial inherent buoyancy and partial inflatable buoyancy might seem a good compromise but they are still fairly bulky and tend to restrict movement. Also they don't provide the full self-righting effect of a lifejacket which will keep your head face-up above water if you are unconscious, as is the case with a fully inflated lifejacket, or one with full inherent buoyancy. The type of lifejacket with gas bottle inflation certainly makes inflation in the water a much easier proposition. Probably the automatic inflation type is the best solution for inflatables and RIBs, but there is always a small risk that if the boat gets inundated with water then the lifejacket may go off inadvertently. With gas bottle inflation there is also the risk that if you partially inflate the life-jacket orally as a precautionary measure, then firing the gas bottle could actually burst the jacket because the pressure will get too high.

So there is no perfect solution to this question of lifejackets. You must make up your own mind about what the risks are, what level of protection you feel is appropriate and what you are prepared to spend. The risk of going overboard unconscious is comparatively small and a fully inflatable lifejacket with gas bottle inflation is probably the best compromise. This is the solution adopted by the RNLI after several years of research but their lifejackets do incorporate automatic inflation. Whatever type you choose it makes a great deal of sense to wear a lifejacket at all times when using inflatables or RIBs. The low freeboard, together with unpredictability and violence of movement make you always at risk of being thrown overboard, and if it does happen, it will happen very suddenly, so you need to be ready for that occurrence.

OTHER AIDS FOR PERSONAL SAFETY
There are various items of personal equipment you can carry in your pockets to give you a further level of protection or at least hasten your recovery from the water. It is possible to get pocket-sized packs of water-proof flares which are fired by a pistol type apparatus to draw attention to your predicament in the water. These flares have a very limited range of visibility and in many countries they require a firearms certificate before you can purchase one. Another possibility is a pack of dye markers

which when released in the water colours a considerable area of water around you, helping to identify your location from the air. The best solution of all is a waterproof VHF radio, so that you can contact the rescue services. Although they are a fairly expensive piece of kit, if you operate a boat on your own you should think seriously about buying a radio of this type because it could represent your only means of calling for help if you get thrown into the water. Another option is an electronic Emergency Position Indicating Radio Beacon (EPIRB) which sends out a distress signal. These can be quite compact and are fully waterproof but they only offer one way communication and you have no knowledge whether your signal has been picked up. Their main advantage is that they have considerable range.

Survival situations

There are a number of scenarios which can be anticipated where inflatables or RIBs could be in difficulty. An engine failure is probably the most obvious one and if you can't fix it then the only solutions open to you are to attract the attention of passing boats, or to call for help with the radio. In the meantime you can put out a sea anchor to prevent the boat drifting too much, particularly if it is drifting in towards an inhospitable shore or on to rocks. A sea anchor will only reduce the drift, it won't prevent it altogether and if you do find yourself getting close to the shore, then it is time to get out the main anchor ready for action. You want the anchor to hold straight away, so pay out the line to virtually its full extent over the side so that it will touch bottom as the water gets shallower. It may not hold initially as the pull on the line is virtually straight up and down, but gradually as the water gets shallower the anchor will start to dig in. The pull on the line will become more horizontal , and eventually with luck, the anchor will hold before you drift on to the rocks. For this type of emergency use you will need a good scope of line; 30 metres length should hold adequately in a water depth of 5 metres even when the wind is blowing strongly on shore.

You could also use the same technique if you wanted to let the boat drift ashore on to a beach where there is a heavy surf. With the motor out of action you would stand a strong risk of capsizing the boat unless you can keep it head on into the waves. The best tactic is to let the boat drift inshore and put out the anchor just before you enter the surf. It requires fine judgement to get the anchor out in the right place because if you put it down too soon, there won't be enough rope to hold the boat as it passes through the lines of surf, and if you leave it too late the boat will be picked up by the surf and probably be capsized by the first wave. Always be on the lookout for that extra big wave which will break further out to sea than the general pattern of waves. Rather than wait till the last minute before throwing out the anchor in this situation, lower it so that it is just touching the sea bed as you drift inshore. It won't hold in this situation, but it will soon get a bite as you slacken a bit more line and this should help you to judge your timing much better. Because of the limited amount of anchor line you have available, this technique is only suitable when there is one or two lines of surf, otherwise you will run out of anchor line long before you get through the surf area.

An alternative is to use a sea anchor for this role, but because the boat will be surging heavily backwards in the surf, the sea anchor and its line need to be very strong to withstand this surge. As we said earlier, the life-raft type of sea anchor with its light line is certainly not adequate for this purpose.

Probably the worst fear of any inflatable or RIB operator is the risk of capsizing. With a small, low speed inflatable this risk could be consider-ably higher than with a fast boat because it is more difficult to position yourself in relation to the waves, and it only needs a breaking wave to come along to tip you over. You can help this to a degree by keeping the boat's bow into the waves which should give you a better chance of sur-vival, but any lapse of concentration could see you in trouble. In a faster boat there should be no real risk of capsizing providing that you maintain concentration, reading the waves all the time, and negotiating rather than trying to do battle with them. (See the chapter Handling Inflatables.)

SELF-RIGHTING SYSTEM
When operating on inshore rescue operations, this risk of capsize is always present, especially in surf, and it was to help in this situation that the self-righting equipment was developed for rigid inflatables. This comprises an air bag mounted on a roll bar with gas bottle inflation. This equipment won't stop the boat capsizing, but it does give you a means of righting the boat once it has capsized. This action is not automatic but requires one of the crew to pull the gas bottle activating trigger to initiate the self-righting, and this should only be done once all the crew have escaped from under-neath the boat and have swum clear. Once the inflation of the righting bag has been initiated, then the righting moment is very quick and could cer-tainly cause injury to any crew caught up with it. Once righted, the crew can climb back on board and hopefully with the sealed engines and the various cut out systems installed in rescue craft, it will be possible to re-start the engine afterwards. The righting bags are usually fitted with a rapid deflation hatch, which allows the bag to be deflated after use, but these are one-shot bags once the air cylinder has been activated, and if one capsize has occurred in the prevailing conditions then there is always the risk of another and so it could be sensible to leave the righting bag inflated until the boat is recovered.

MANUAL RECOVERY AFTER A CAPSIZE
The vast proportion of inflatables and RIBs do not have self-righting systems, so a capsize in one of these means that any efforts to right the boat have to be done manually. With small inflatables it is possible to right the boat by tying a line on one side of the boat, leading this over the upturned bottom and then standing on the opposite tube to where the line

An inflation test on a self-righting bag on a rigid inflatable. The frame also acts as a mounting point for navigation lights, antennae and mooring cleats.

is attached, leaning backwards and using your body weight to pull the boat up and over. If the side of the boat you are trying to lift is kept upwind, the task will be easier because once the wind gets under the boat it will help you to complete the righting task. If you capsize in a small rowing inflatable your first priority is to make sure that the oars don't drift away otherwise you will be adrift once the boat has been righted.

Trying to right a boat which is anything over 5 metres in length is probably an impossible task, one which will be made even harder if powerful
engines are fitted. The chances are, too, that it will be impossible to re-start
the engines again because they will not be protected in the way that the
engines on self-righting boats are. In this situation you will be better off
calling for assistance by any means available rather than expending the
effort trying to right the boat. You can usually sit quite comfortably on the
upturned boat, particularly if you rig a rope across the bottom to give you
something to hold on to.

RESCUING CASUALTIES
You may be the boat that is called upon to help other people. With an
inflatable or RIB you have a boat which comes close to the ideal rescue vessel, certainly for going alongside and getting people off a boat in difficulties. The lee side is obviously the best place to go alongside because you
have a degree of protection from the stricken vessel, and the inflatable
tube will act as a fender.

Trying to pick up someone from the water is much more difficult. Even
with the low freeboard and the stability of an inflatable this is never an
easy task and you must always bear in mind the risk of inflicting injury to
the person in the water from a turning propeller. Despite the need for
speed, it is wise to slow down before you get to a casualty so that you
make the approach gently. This will give you time to assess the situation
but also will be a lot less frightening for the casualty in the water than racing towards him at high speed. Aim to stop the boat about 1 metre away
from the casualty up to windward, take the engine out of gear and let the
boat drift towards the casualty. You will need to get hold of the person in
the water quickly to prevent him drifting under the boat. If there are two
of you on board then you should be able to get hands underneath the casualty's armpits and literally drag him over the air tube. If you are alone you
will need to pass a rope round his chest under the arms and tie a non-slip
knot such as a bowline. A further method which may be worth trying
especially if he has sustained injuries to chest or arms is to pass a loop of
rope (with the ends secured onboard) under the torso and legs, as he lies
horizontally in the water parallel to the boat, then simply haul up on the
loop to roll him over the air tube into the boat. This is known as parbuck-
ling.

Once on board avoid the temptation to rush for the shore, first assess
the condition of the casualty. If he is conscious, find a comfortable place
for him, preferably protected from the wind, perhaps wedging him in
position with lifejackets. Check for any apparent injuries before heading,
at a moderate speed, for harbour. If the casualty is unconscious, the first
thing you must do is check his breathing and give artificial ventilation if
necessary before doing anything else. It is vital to try and restore breathing immediately, but it may be possible to drive the boat at slow speed
towards the shore whilst carrying out the resuscitation procedure. The
value of a radio in these conditions cannot be over-emphasised so that you

can contact the coastguard who will alert the rescue services to quickly provide a helicopter or lifeboat to take over responsibility for the casualty.

TOWING

Towing another boat with an inflatable is difficult because it has very little grip on the water and the towed craft will tend to steer the tower whereas the vee bottom of a rigid inflatable is better for this task. It is possible to tow boats with both types of craft although anything larger than a dinghy will have to be towed at very slow speed. One of the biggest problems is finding a strong enough tow point to make fast a tow line; the best solution is to try and spread the weight of the tow line between two or three attachment points. You can use handholds or lifting points if there is no towing post but spread the load between them and at all costs keep the tow line clear of the engine and the propeller.

FLARES

You should carry flares on board to attract attention if you get into trouble. However, you need to be careful when using flares in an inflatable boat. Once they have been fired off, hand flares tend to spew out a lot of hot ash, which will rapidly burn through an inflatable tube. If you do have to use a hand flare, make sure you hold it well out to leeward so that the ash will blow off down wind and not out over the tube. With parachute flares, the problem is not so great because once the rocket is fired, the exhaust rapidly disappears away from the boat up into the air and the risk. of anything burning is negligible.

This Tinker inflatable has an inflatable canopy which gives the boat many of the characteristics of a liferaft.

INFLATABLES AS LIFERAFTS

Some inflatables used as yacht tenders also double up as emergency liferafts. This could be an acceptable practice for yachts operating close to land, but it should be borne in mind that however well it is converted for its liferaft role, no inflatable can fully meet the survival requirements built into a liferaft. One of the major areas of difference is the fitting of stability pockets into the bottom of the liferaft which helps reduce the possibility of a capsize. Liferafts also tend to have an inflatable floor which provides good insulation between cold sea water and the occupants inside the liferaft. It will also have a canopy with supporting tubes to give protection from the weather.

However, an inflatable boat can provide a viable means of escape in an emergency and some are fitted with CO_2 cylinders to give rapid inflation when required for use. Unless relief valves are fitted, any automatic inflation system must be used with care because it can lead to over-inflation and possible bursting of the tube due to excess pressure. It is possible to get an inflatable protective cover for some types, and this will improve the chances of survival of the occupants when the craft is used for its emergency role. These covers are usually inflated by hand which means operating the bellows once you have abandoned ship and you will also need to have a grab bag handy with items such as flares, sea anchor, knife and other emergency equipment. The authorities tend to frown on the use of inflatables as substitute liferafts and rarely sanction their use where there is a mandatory requirement for liferafts, but they can provide a viable alternative in many situations provided that you understand the limitations involved and the risks inherent in using an inflatable rather than a fully effective liferaft.

CHAPTER 9

▪▪▪▪▪▪▪▪▪▪

LAUNCHING AND TRANSPORTING

This chapter divides into two main sections: one covering the situation when the boat is carried on board a mother ship, whether it be a yacht, an offshore standby vessel, patrol boat or naval vessel and the other covers transporting the boat by road. Both of these areas are tailor made for rigid inflatable operations but they also introduce some limitations, particularly when launching from a mother ship. Launch and recovery, whether it is from ship or shore not only creates specific problems which we will look at here, but they also serve to widen the application of the boats as well. In both of these areas there is considerable scope for further development.

Launching and recovery from a mother ship

The techniques here will vary considerably, depending on whether the boat can easily be handled by manpower or whether you need mechanical power. In its simplest form the yacht tender can be launched over the rail by one person, and recovered in the same way and the operation is certainly made easier if the rails can be removed. These small boats are generally light enough for one person to handle quite easily. Two people, one each side of the boat, make the job even easier, but in either case make sure that the painter line is made fast before you put the boat overboard otherwise you may see your tender drifting away. You will want to keep the inside of the inflatable as dry as possible, so when launching try and prevent water from slopping over the transom as the boat goes into the water. There is generally plenty of buoyancy to keep the water out, but in lively sea conditions try to launch on the lee side or at least where the water is less active.

DAVITS AND OTHER STOWAGE
Larger yacht tenders which cannot be handled quite so easily by hand or where there is less space for stowage on deck are often carried in stowage in davits across the transom. This means that lifting points for the davit attachment are required in the boat. For an inflatable, these are usually attached to the transom and to the forward floors or air tubes, whilst for a rigid inflatable they are incorporated into the rigid section of the hull usually at the transom and forward. Two or three lifting points are generally

An inflatable tender stowed partially inflated on a yacht. There should be enough buoyancy left to keep you afloat if you have to abandon ship in a hurry. Webbing straps are better than ropes for lashing the boat in place.

adequate; to launch lower the boat into the water and to recover you simply hook on and hoist it out of the water.

While the operation of launch and recovery is quite straightforward, actually stowing the boat securely in the davits may not be quite so easy. It is vitally important that you secure the boat so that it doesn't move and cause chafe against the air tubes. The usual method is to have webbing straps around the boat and have these secured to the davit or back on board. These straps work well provided the air tubes keep their pressure but with variations in temperature the pressure can vary and any reduction can lead to the securing straps slackening off and the boat starting to move in its stowage. This means that you will need to check the stowage every hour or so at sea to make sure the tender is secure, particularly in lively sea conditions.

An alternative to using davits, which do tend to be vulnerable when you are manoeuvring in marinas, is to stow the boat on the bathing platform aft. A variety of ingenious systems are available but one of the simplest hinges one side of the boat, with special attachments on the air tube, into matching attachments on the outer edge of the bathing platform. This allows the other side of the boat to be pulled in using the hinge as a fulcrum, and stowed flat against the transom. It makes for a secure, tight stowage and provides a very practical and space saving solution. Stowages of this type are equally applicable to inflatables and RIBs but RIBs lend themselves better to davit stowage because securing strops can be attached to points on the hulls so that the pressure in the inflation tubes will not affect the stability of the stowage.

Stowage space for the inflatable tender on this motor yacht has been found inside the transom via a hinged door which folds open to create the launching ramp.

On larger sailing yachts, stowage space is often created under the aft cockpit or above the engine compartment. Creating this form of 'garage' for the tender is a relatively new development and the stowage incorporates an hydraulically controlled hatch in the transom which, when open, forms a launching ramp for the boat. A slipway or rollers are incorporated into this ramp and also into the boat stowage, and a small electrical or hydraulic hoist is used to launch and recover the boat. For launching, the hoist is simply slackened off and the boat runs down the slipway created by the hatch cover and into the water. On recovery the bow of the boat is nudged into the slipway, the hoist attached, and the boat recovered promptly and quickly.

PROFESSIONAL STOWAGE SYSTEMS
On large yachts, this type of launch and recovery is generally carried out in calm conditions, often when the mother ship is at anchor. A similar but much more rugged system has been developed for patrol boat and lifeboat applications which allows launch and recovery in open water conditions. Here the designers are much less interested in the aesthetics of the situation, and much more concerned with its practicality. The boat is usually carried on board in an angled recess in the deck where it sits snugly, usually just below deck level. The angled stowage is fitted with rollers and a transom gate which closes off the stowage area when the boat is not in use. The stowage can be lowered hydraulically to form an extension of the slipway, which allows the boat to slide directly into the water. Recovery is similar to that used on yachts with the bow being nudged into the slipway

and the engines kept running ahead until the hoist is attached and tightened. The main difference between such a system and the yacht systems is that the hinged transom gate has to be constructed much more ruggedly because the stresses of recovery in the open sea can be very high. The advantages of this ramp system are that launch and recovery can be carried out successfully in quite difficult conditions, because by steaming ahead the mother ship creates an effective lee at the stern and these relatively stable waters make the recovery a practical proposition. The rigid inflatable is simply driven up through the wake of the mother ship and held in position under engine power on the bottom end of the ramp, whilst the hoist line is attached, and the boat is then winched up into its stowage. For both launch and recovery the crew are on board and the boat is ready to go as soon as it is launched. An essential for this type of stowage is that the stowage recess is made self-draining so that large quantities of water are not retained which could affect stability. Simple large drains in the transom are the answer, usually closed off by outside flap valves.

Ideally for this type of launch and recovery operation the boat should be water jet powered so that there are no protruding elements below the bottom of the boat, but the system can be used with outboard or stern drive powered boats. The boat is held on the slipway once the transom is just clear of the end of it so the engine can be lowered and started prior to launch. On recovery there has to be a similar pause while the engine is tilted, but in both circumstances the boat is securely held on the slipway and launch and recovery should not present any problems. Obviously good teamwork is necessary for the system to be effective but a growing number of patrol boats are adopting this method particularly where launch and recovery of the boarding boat has to be a regular occurrence, such as in fishery protection or customs operations.

On large yachts a davit launch system is fairly simple to engineer because launch and recovery tends to take place either in sheltered anchorages or in harbour when the mother ship is not rolling or pitching. Here the designer will tend to be more concerned with the aesthetic appeal of the crane or davit, rather than its launching effectiveness, but for the professional user it is the launch and recovery system which effectively limits the conditions in which the boat can be used. Recovery is the most critical part of the operation and one of the difficulties experienced by most professional users is trying to gauge whether the conditions are suitable for a recovery operation and this can only be put to the test only after the boat has been launched and is committed.

Davit systems for launching and recovering rigid inflatables tend to be heavy and cumbersome so that they are only suitable for large ships. Even then they offer little control over the movement of the boat when it is hanging on the end of a single point lift until the boat is up and safe in its stowage. Designers now tend to favour the more versatile crane launch system using hydraulic knuckle or extending boom cranes which can be used for a variety of other purposes on the mother ship in addition to their

A launch and recovery crane for a rigid inflatable. The secondary arm which hooks over the side of the boat controls the boat's movement whilst it is airborne and makes launch and recovery a one-man operation.

function of launching and recovering the boat. The problem with these cranes is that once the boat is hoisted out of its stowage on the single point lift of the crane, it can swing in all directions and it requires ropes from the boat to try and reduce this movement which can cause damage particularly to outboards and stern drives. Light rigid inflatables can be controlled by ropes but it does require increased manpower for the launch and recovery operation, something not always available with the limited crew on board some of these vessels. With the heavier rigid inflatable, control by manpower becomes more difficult and the only satisfactory solution is a fully integrated launch and recovery system which keeps the movement of the boat firmly under control whatever the sea state. One such system has a metal frame attached to the head of the crane, and once the boat is lifted from its stowage it engages into this frame so that all movement is controlled until the boat is swung out over the side and lowered out of the frame and into the water. Once over the side the boat can be kept close into the ship's side to control its movement to a considerable degree. The lowering of the boat should be as rapid as possible to reduce the time when the boat is suspended and has to be controlled in the air. Similarly on recovery, the lifting wires are hooked on and the boat hoisted clear of the water where it engages with the frame on the crane and is then under full control whilst it is transferred from the ship's side into its stowage. The frame can be rotated under hydraulic power so that the heading of the boat can be varied to match up with the stowage. Such a system provides a very practical solution to the problems of launch and recovery and makes the whole operation controllable by the crane driver.

With this type of launch and recovery, the lifting point attachments in the boat should be engineered to improve safety and to match the lifting system. The three or four point webbing lifting slings which are often used can be extremely dangerous as they can snap tight without warning as the boat rises and falls alongside the mother ship. A crew member has to use two hands to hook on these straps: one to hold the lifting wire hook, and the other to hold the connecting ring of the slings, so that when hooking on he is not holding on to the boat for his own security. This crewman can be at considerable risk both from being catapulted overboard and from trapping his fingers in the lifting hook. The whole operation, using these flexible slings, is fraught with danger and the slings are also left lying in the bottom of the boat after launching where they can get in the way.

There is a move towards the use of what might be termed 'rigid slings' which is a metal tubular frame constructed in the boat with the lifting point at its apex. This is normally fitted with a quick release connector which is controlled from inside the boat, allowing the coxswain to release the lifting wire when he thinks fit so that there are no components of the lifting apparatus to fall down on his head unlike with flexible slings. For recovery the crewman first gets hold of the lifting wire with its hook with one hand as the boat comes alongside, leaving him with the other hand free to hold on to the lifting frame. In this way he is fully in control of the situation and can clip the hook in quickly to allow hoisting to begin.

The less time the boat spends alongside the mother ship, once it has been launched or is being recovered, the better because it is in a vulnerable situation. The mother ship will normally have headway on when the launch and recovery operation is taking place because this helps to reduce the motion of the ship and also gives the boat better control when coming in alongside for the recovery operation. For recovery it is probably adequate for the helmsman to hold the boat alongside using engine power while the crewman hooks in the recovery wire, but such a system may not always work for launching. Here, as soon as the boat is launched it will tend to drift astern because of the headway of the mother ship, and unless the lifting wire is released quickly the boat can turn broad side on and be pulled along sideways by the lifting wire creating a situation which can rapidly get worse unless prompt action is taken. Ideally then for the launching operation at least, a painter should be run out from the bow to a point well forward of the launching point and this will serve to hold the boat in position alongside while the hoist wire is being disconnected. Such a system is essential if a quick release hook is not used but even with a quick release hook which can be released under load, it is a good safety precaution to use a painter, and is essential if the engine of the boat cannot be started until it is in the water. The painter can be taken up back on board the mother ship when it is let go rather than stowed in the boat itself. This means that you need one more crew member to handle the painter on board the mother ship but this is a sound and seamanlike way of boat launching and again it requires teamwork, practice and an understanding of procedures if the whole operation is to go smoothly.

There has been a tendency by professional users who launch and recover rigid inflatables in the open sea to buy the boat and the hoisting equipment separately, and then try to marry the two together. For efficiency, there is a need for these two items to be fully integrated and the whole system needs to be carefully planned and engineered if it is to work successfully in difficult conditions. Again it is worth repeating that it is during the launch and recovery operations that the crew are most at risk and if effective use is to be made of the boarding boat in difficult sea conditions then this aspect of launch and recovery needs to be well planned and practiced.

Transport by road

Now we will switch to wheeled transport of inflatables and RIBs. The simplest method here is to fold the boat up and put it in the boot of the car. This can be done with smaller inflatables and allows you to transport the boat at high speed with virtually no risk involved. The only thing you need to consider is the possibility of chafe when the car is moving but a bag is often supplied for this type of boat and this should prevent wear and tear during transport. The boat and engine takes up a lot of space and you do have to go through the chore of inflating and assembling the boat when you arrive at the launching site. Because of this, many owners of small inflatables and RIBs will carry their boats on the roof of the car; this is a practical proposition for boats up to around four metres in length.

You can put the boat directly on top of the roof but there will inevitably be a degree of movement between the boat and the car roof which can lead to the paint being scratched, particularly if there are any protruding parts on the inflatable tube. A special roof rack is, therefore, the best solution, and this provides you with a way of securing the boat, although ropes leading from the boat to the front and back of the car are a good back up because the wind stresses on the boat can be quite high. The boat is best stowed upside-down on the roof where its shape will tend to offer less wind resistance; the wind passing over the boat will tend to press it down on to the roof rather than lift it up. If carried the right way up there is always the risk of the boat collecting water if it rains, and this will add extra weight and stress to both the boat and the car. In this case the drain plug, if there is one, should always be left out. Rigid inflatables tend to have transom drains, so any rain water which collects can quickly drain out, but do make sure that these are open. When securing a rigid inflatable, the securing lines or straps should always be made fast to the rigid part of the hull; with an inflatable you don't have much choice and variations in temperature could affect the tube pressure and loosen the straps. With any type of boat transported in this way it is a sensible precaution to stop every hour or so and check the security of the boat and its lashings.

Trailer types

For boats of four metres and over, the weight and the awkwardness of handling on and off the roof makes a trailer a better proposition. Trailer costs can be as high as 20–25% of the overall cost of the boat and you need to bear this in mind when developing your budget but don't be tempted to economise. The best quality trailers are hot-dipped galvanised steel. Ungalvanised trailers will need an annual re-paint and careful monitoring for corrosion.

There are three types of trailer to consider for inflatables and RIBs: the adjustable backbone trailer, the break-back and the 'piggy-back'. The first type requires total wheel immersion at most sites. The break-back has a double chassis; by removing a pin, the rear section of the trailer hinges down to form a ramp for launching the boat. On a slipway with a reasonable angle, this can allow the boat to be launched without putting the trailer wheels in the water and can make recovery easier. The 'piggy-back' is another version which helps to prevent the wheels from being immersed. With this type there is a small launching trailer carried on top of the road trailer. Although this will protect your road wheel bearings, recovery is hard work without assistance from your vehicle so restricting the use of a 'piggy-back' to small boats.

A trailer for an inflatable needs to be of the flat-bed type in order to

The simplest form of road trailer for a RIB. An inflatable would require more support.

spread the weight of the boat. Padded wooden planks fixed to a 'backbone' with a single axle will form a basic style. Another design takes the form of a cradle of tubular metal which supports the air tubes on either side. It should also have support for keel and transom, particularly if the outboard is carried in place.

RIBs require support for the rigid hull, which is best provided by rubber rollers. If the boat is correctly positioned, it should not be possible to turn any of the rollers independently but they should all turn when the boat is moved on the trailer.

Tow vehicles

Unless you are towing one of the larger RIBs, the average modern family saloon of 1600 cc or over will be able to cope with reasonable towing distances provided that hills are not excessive and the slipways are not too steep.

Towing a trailer makes you subject to a great number of rules and regulations about size, weight and speed. Details of these regulations can be obtained in the UK from the HMSO. It is generally considered, for safety, that the towed load should not exceed 90% of the vehicle's kerb weight. Most vehicle manufacturers will recommend towing weights for their various models so check with them if you are unsure. If you do not know the combined weight of your trailer and boat, take the rig to your local public weigh-bridge. It is important to establish the weight because if exceeded, it may invalidate your insurance (You should tell the insurance companies, for both car and boat, if you are intending to tow.) If the load exceeds 750 kg or is over half the kerb weight of the tow vehicle, the trailer must have brakes.

You will also need to fit a towing hitch to your car with a plug-in electrical system for a lighting board on the trailer.

If you are in the market for a potential tow vehicle, it is well worth considering an automatic transmission as it will make your job easier. The torque converter in the automatic gearbox gives more power in the lower gears so giving better control on slipways and hills with less chance of stalling. Also, the almost inevitable weekend hold-ups on motorways and approaches to holiday destinations become considerably less tiring and stressful with an automatic transmission.

If you have a manual transmission, do make sure that your clutch is up to it – very slight slipping under ordinary conditions will be very noticeable under a heavy load.

Pay special attention to your brakes, especially if towing an unbraked trailer. Have them checked before travelling because, as with the clutch, any wear will become very obvious when you are under load.

Preparing for the road

The trailer will need to be fitted with a removable lighting board which has brake lights, indicators and reflectors conforming to EC regulations.

Once you have connected up the lead to the socket on the tow bar, get some-one to operate the lights on the car so you can check that the lighting board is working properly. Whilst at the rear, make sure that any projection, such as the prop, is safely covered. If the projection is in excess of a metre it is a legal requirement in the EC to make it clearly visible. A bright fluorescent padded bag offers protection and makes other motorists aware of it.

Although this may seem obvious, make sure that the boat is *securely* tied to the trailer. You can use the painter to secure the bow to the cross-bar near the jockey wheel. If you have a winch, this will serve to keep the boat in its forward position if the tape or cable is wound up fully. For holding the boat down on the trailer safely, the easiest system is probably two to three webbing straps tightened with rachet buckles. With a RIB, all attach-ments should be made to the rigid part of the hull. If you use rope for securing the boat, make sure that it is well padded where it touches the tubes to avoid chafe. If you are travelling for a long distance, it is a good idea to stop after an hour's travelling to check the fastenings. Bear in mind that the boat will probably suffer more wear and tear and stress on the road than it will ever do out to sea.

Take all loose gear out of the boat before trailing in case it bounces out. If you do leave anything in the boat, make sure that it is firmly lashed in place; a cover is useful to keep rain out and to keep the boat clean and it will also help to keep loose items safe.

CHECKING THE BALANCE
The balance of the boat on the trailer needs to be carefully checked; whilst the trailer should be front heavy, you should still be able to lift up the front when the boat is loaded to show that there will not be too much downward force on the tow hitch – this will affect the handling of the car, particularly when going downhill. If you can lift the front of the trailer quite easily, it will mean that there is a weight of about 30 lb (13.6 kg) on the tow hitch. If there is more weight than this, the boat should be moved aft on the trailer; less and the boat must be shifted forward. If the required change in balance is small, it can often be achieved by moving fuel tanks or other items of equipment to a different stowage place inside the boat. When the final position has been determined, make sure that the supports are properly adjusted.

Towing to the launch site

If it is properly loaded, balanced and secured, towing an inflatable should not prove too difficult for an experienced driver, but here are a few tips which may make your journey safer and easier:

- Check out your route in advance, avoiding difficult country lanes, tiny villages and steep hills where possible. Get a reliable person to navigate if you are visiting a new launch site so that you are free to concentrate on your driving.

- Keep your driving as smooth as possible; avoid heavy braking and sudden gear changes.
- Give yourself plenty of braking room - the extra weight will make your brakes far less responsive; be especially careful if you are towing an unbraked trailer.
- Don't forget your width - allow extra room for passing parked cars and overtaking.
- Don't forget your length - take your corners slightly wider to avoid clipping the curb. When overtaking slower vehicles, remember to allow two car lengths to avoid cutting up the vehicle that you are passing.
- Reverse very slowly with someone positioned behind to give you directions. If you haven't towed before, it is an idea to practice reversing in an empty car park before you need to carry out this manoeuvre on a busy slipway.
- Make sure that you have good rear vision.
- Beware when leaving filling station forecourts, it is all too easy to leave a trail of destruction behind you!

Having successfully negotiated the urban hazards and reached the apparent safety of the motorway you may then be tempted to relax and put your foot down a little. Be careful when increasing your speed, however, because if you travel too fast you will start to 'snake'. The trailer will begin to swing from side to side, gradually gathering momentum and affecting your stability. It is also very alarming for other road users, especially those overtaking you. High winds will add to this effect together with the slipstreams of commercial vehicles. Never be tempted to brake when this happens, just ease off the throttle until the snaking subsides.

Another towing phenomena to be aware of is 'pitching'. This occurs when the load is incorrectly balanced giving rise to a see-saw effect. Too little, or conversely, too much weight on the nose will cause pitching, or it can start when a fuel tank or another heavy item shifts its position in the boat. If you experience pitching, stop and adjust the loading or you will have a very uncomfortable ride and the rear suspension of your vehicle could be weakened.

Launching and recovery

If you have not launched before, do not wait until a busy bank holiday to make your debut on a busy slip with queues of waiting boats. Take a couple of friends down to your nearest slip at a quiet time mid-week and have a practice. You may find that your boat and trailer will have interesting behaviour patterns when on a slip so it is as well to know about these in advance. Here are a few launching tips:

- Arrive at your launch site early and have two or three helpers available, well briefed.

Preparing for launching. It is much easier to load all the equipment you need in the boat before putting it in the water.

- Before you move on to the slip, remove the lashings, bag for the prop and lighting board and stow them safely in the car.
- If you have a winch, check that this is working freely.
- Connect fuel lines and battery to the engine; see that the engine is well tilted up to avoid catching the prop on the slip.
- Make sure that the trailer and car are in line as you back down the slip otherwise you may run off the side. Have someone stationed to one side at the bottom of the slip to tell you when to stop.
- If you need to disconnect the trailer to push it into the water, put the handbrake on and have two people steady the trailer to prevent it from running away prematurely.
- Position someone in the water to hold the painter while the car and trailer are being parked unless the boat can be temporarily moored out of the way of other slip users.
- Before firing up the engine, ensure that there is sufficient depth of water to cover the water intakes.

With recovery, the main difficulty is positioning the boat correctly on the trailer; don't allow yourself to be rushed if the slip is busy. Remember that it is a lot easier to float the boat into the right position than to try to man-handle it on dry land; you then run the risk of damaging the keel. A winch and rollers should make light work of recovery as once it is lined up, the boat should come up straight. With an inflatable on a flat-bed trailer, you will have to keep a good eye on the positioning both fore and aft and sideways to get the weight evenly spread. Make sure that the engine is on full tilt and that the drain in the transom is open to allow any water to run out as the boat comes up the slip – you don't want the added weight of a few gallons of seawater on the way home. As the car starts up the slip (a good test for the clutch) you will find that it may become light at the front as the weight of the trailer and boat bears down on the back axle. This can be overcome by someone sitting on the bonnet to help give better grip but make sure that they sit to one side and slide off as soon as firm traction is achieved.

Road trailers seldom operate effectively over open beaches even if you leave your car behind and manhandle the trailer down to the shore. For beach work, whether it is over sand or gravel, you need wider tyres with lower pressures than you would for road use, but it is still difficult to push a boat over soft sand or gravel and this method of launching should only be considered if the boat is relatively small and light. You may find it easier to carry the boat rather than to wheel it, and much will depend on how firm the conditions are on the beach, and how many people you have available. Obviously, if your tow vehicle has four-wheel drive, then you may have more flexibility in taking the vehicle out on to the beach, if this is permitted. If you use this method of launching regularly, it can be sensible to consider having a towing hitch fitted on the front of the vehicle as well as the rear, as it is easier to see what is going on.

Trailer maintenance

Maintenance of the launching trailer is vital if it is going to be reliable. Take the time to grease any exposed threads on the roller adjustments, the clamp for the jockey wheel and the ball hitch socket which conneects with the car. Even though you won't need to adjust them once the boat is set in position, the time may come when you will need to change the setting and greasing will help to keep them moving. The jockey wheel clamp, in particular, gets a lot of use so keep it in good order. When on the road, ensure the jockey wheel is clamped up as far as it will go – tie it up with a rope in case the clamp comes loose. Before launching, remember to take the lighting board off the trailer if it is likely to go in the water. Salt water is very corrosive when it comes into contact with electrical systems and they rarely work after immersion.

The normal galvanised trailer chassis will resist corrosion pretty well and shouldn't cause any trouble. It is the wheel bearings which suffer most from immersion in water, particularly salt water. Ideally, you should launch the boat without putting the wheels in the water, but in most cases this is not a practical proposition, so do make sure that your trailer either has fully sealed bearings which can stand up to this treatment, or at least grease nipples which can be used to grease the bearings immediately after use. If water finds its way into the bearing, corrosion will start in a very short space of time, leading to bearing failure on the road. Water ingress shouldn't be a problem with modern fully sealed bearings but seals often get old and worn through neglect or through using the trailer on a sandy beach. Apart from regular checking of the seal, if you can see it, these bearings only need to be stripped and packed with fresh grease once a year. If the wheel bearings are fitted with grease nipples, use these to pump fresh grease into the bearings every time the trailer has been immersed in order to force out any water.

Trailers for the professionals

For professional use, a variety of specialised launching trailers have been developed and rescue boats often use these. Some professionals who use road transport to get their boat close to the scene of an incident will want trailers which provide a simple, smooth launching operation and the tilting trailer, which allows you to vary the angle of the trailer, can provide a useful solution. For beach launches and the recovery of larger rigid inflatables, the RNLI has developed a self-propelled trailer which uses hydrostatic propulsion in each wheel. Capable of operating over rough and soft terrain, these launch trailers are simply driven into the water to a depth where the engine of the boat can be started. The trailer holds the boat securely in place with its bow pointing seaward, with the full complement of crew on board. Then the engine is started, put into gear and the boat is driven out of the trailer. The trailer has a Y-shaped chassis so that the engine or engines are kept clear during the launching process. For recovery, a catching net is rigged in the trailer into which the boat is driven at speed. The net brings the boat to a halt and the trailer then drives out of the water where the boat is reversed ready for launching again. This is a specialised type of launch and recovery system, but it does give some indication of what can be done when the circumstances demand it.

CHAPTER 10

CARE AND REPAIR

The very nature of an inflatable boat and its ability to bounce off quays and jetties and other boats tends to make it the subject of abuse. These boats often operate off beaches where the wear and tear tends to be exaggerated because of the sand and shingle. In general, inflatables and rigid inflatables lead a hard life, so that both the maintenance and repair of these boats is a very important factor in maintaining reliability. Knowing how to repair the boat can often get you out of trouble when something goes wrong in areas remote from service. The need for emergency repairs may be reduced if you use the boat carefully but as an owner you should be capable of carrying out basic repair work. Make sure that you understand your boat, know how and when damage and wear is likely to occur and how to keep the boat in sound condition.

Full maintenance work can normally be done during an annual check when you carry out any necessary painting, varnishing and the re-gluing of any areas which have come adrift. However, it is well worth going through a quick routine check every time the boat comes back in from the sea. In this way you will discover any damage or wear before it gets serious, but, equally importantly, you will be secure in the knowledge that the boat is ready for sea next time you come to use it.

Regular maintenance

WASHING DOWN
The first thing to do is to wash down the boat thoroughly with fresh water. This gets rid of all the salt and can remove grit and other contamination from inside the boat. You will need to position the boat so that the water can drain out of it and with a rigid inflatable you probably only need to chock the boat with the bow slightly raised so that water can drain out through the transom. With an inflatable you may have to stand the boat virtually on end to wash it out if there is no transom drain. Dirt and grit inside the boat is very abrasive, particularly if abrasive material gets into tiny corners of the boat, particularly between the area where the air tube is attached to the rigid deck or the flexible floor of the boat, it can rub the neoprene skin off the fabric making it susceptible to air leaks. On inflatables, the situation is probably worsened by the fact that the wooden floors

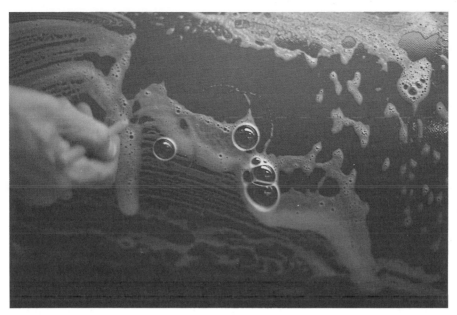

Testing for leaks in the air tube. A chinagraph pencil is used to mark the area after soapy water is brushed on and the bubbles indicate the leak.

fit tightly into this corner between the air tube and the fabric floor but there is always a small enough gap left to allow the grains of sand to work their way in. Wear and tear in these corners can be quite rapid unless you wash the boat out every time you come in from sea. At the same time check that there are no pebbles or larger items trapped in these corners.

Rather than just hosing the boat out with fresh water first wash it down with a bucket of water containing mild detergent, perhaps washing-up liquid. This will remove any grease or other contaminates from the rubber fabric. This hand washing also means that you will look at the tube a bit more carefully and you may discover patches or tapes starting to lift on the air tube. Using detergent on the surface of the air tubes could also indicate any air leaks by the group of bubbles which will gather round the leak. Any defects of this type should receive attention at the time rather than be left to get worse.

ROUTINE CHECKS

Once you have washed out the boat, then take the time to have a quick look around to check fittings and fixtures. On a rigid inflatable look inside the console to make sure there is no damp on the electrics and if there are any exposed connections, then a spray with a silicone grease aerosol will help keep corrosion at bay. Any moving parts such as catches should be treated with the same aerosol spray, but don't use it on the air valves in the tubes or other threaded components because it will tend to attract dust and grit which may make it very difficult to operate the screw thread. If there is a drain plug in the transom of a rigid inflatable, then remove it to check that no water has got inside the rigid section of the hull. Such drains are normally fitted to quality RIBs, but if your boat doesn't have one, then think about drilling a suitable hole as low down as possible in the transom, clear of the stiffening frames to allow drainage. The hole need be no more than half a centimetre across and it can be closed off with a wooden or rubber bung which is hammered tightly into the hole with a suitable sealant although a proper screwed bung is preferable.

This routine check should include the engine as well. It is best to do this when you come ashore rather than before you go out to sea because then you know that everything is secure and working rather than discover a problem just before you want to launch. With outboard engines this checking routine simply means taking off the engine cover and looking for loose wires and corrosion or any drips of fuel indicating leaks. Check hoses and connections with a simple wiggle of the pipe; if the fuel filter has a glass bowl, check that there is clear, clean fuel showing in the glass. If all looks well then spray the outside of the engine, but particularly the electrical system, with the silicone grease aerosol, put the hood back and hopefully you should have an engine which will start up first time when you next come to use it.

With inboard engines the installation is more complex, but you are looking around the engine compartment for the same sort of problems: check that electrical wires are not chafing, that there is no corrosion on terminals, that water and fuel pipes are intact and there are no oil leaks, and that everything looks in order. Obviously you check the oil and water levels but this is really something you should also do just before you go to sea as part of your final check. Even though the engine has a fresh water cooling system, which in turn is cooled by sea water as is generally the case, it can pay to wash it through with fresh water by connecting a hose to the water inlet system and running the engine so that any salt contamination in the engine is replaced by fresh water. Don't run the engine unless the hose is connected and there is a good supply of water, otherwise you could quickly burn out the water pump and possibly damage the flexible exhaust. Outboard engines can benefit by being run with fresh water passing through the cooling system, and it is possible to get a clamp which fits over the normal water intake of the engine and blocks it off allowing a hose to be connected for this purpose. (See Engine Cooling page 51.)

Annual maintenance and repairs

This routine maintenance should not take more than 10 or 15 minutes but at the end of the season, or when the boat is taken out of service, you need to do a much more thorough job. Even so it should not take more than half a day to go through the boat in detail, and a full day if there is any repair or maintenance work to be carried out. Whether you have an inflatable or a RIB, you need to strip the boat down as far as possible so that you can get access to and inspect the parts which are not normally visible. With inflatables this means removing all the floor boards and other portable fittings, whereas with a rigid inflatable it may be possible to remove the console and open up the hatch covers or deck panels.

You can divide the inspection into two parts, one for the rigid areas such as floor boards, transoms and the rigid hull in the case of RIBs, and the second is for the air tubes and flexible fabric components. For the floor boards and transoms of an inflatable, the inspection is largely a question of making sure that there are no splits or cracks and, perhaps more importantly, no sharp edges caused through wear and tear which could lead to a puncture of the air tube. On inflatables the main problem area is likely to be the stringers which lock the floorboards together, because these can come under considerable strain and they also bear directly on to the inflatable tubes, so they are a critical part of the boat. On the transom, check that the engine plates are secure, that there has not been any movement between the outboard engine and the transom which has led to wear, and that the fabric flanges which attach the transom to the air tube are intact and have not started to peel away. Particularly important on an inflatable is the area of the floor fabric where it joins on to the transom. This takes a lot of wear and tear and is where you are most likely to find the rubber coating worn off the fabric. If the boat has a wooden keelson you may find similar wear in this area. If all looks intact and in reasonable condition then maintenance can simply be a question of painting or varnishing if the components are of wood, or if they are metal or GRP then there is probably nothing that you need do except reassemble them.

If you are varnishing any wooden components, then thoroughly rub down the woodwork with sandpaper to get a clean, even surface finish. You will need to apply probably four or five coats of a good quality marine varnish (two-part polyurethane varnish is the most durable) to produce a finish which is going to stand up to a season's use. . Time spent on getting the varnished wood back into top condition will be repaid in the longer life it will have in the harsh sea environment. Any damage to the rigid components should be carefully repaired or the parts replaced. If engine mounting holes in the transom have become elongated, then existing holes can be filled with wooden plugs and epoxy filler and then new holes drilled as required. Most minor damage to floors and other components can be repaired by similar use of epoxy filler which is applied to the damaged area after it has been cleaned up and then the surface is ground down to match the original.

Repairing hull damage on RIBs

With the rigid hull of a RIB the first thing to do is to go over the surface carefully, inspecting every square centimetre of it for chips and scratches. This is best done by rubbing your hand over the surface; you will often be able to feel chips and scratches before you can see them, particularly if they don't extent right through the gel coat to the laminate underneath. Mark these areas with a waterproof felt tip pen as you find them, then look at each one more carefully. You can tell if it is just the gel coat which has been damaged when you see the same colour right through the scratch or chip. Then you simply lightly grind out the cavity with an emery disc in an electric drill or even with emery paper used by hand, and fill up the hole with matching gel coat which can usually be obtained from the boat manufacturer. To complete the job, you then grind the gel coat filling flush with the surrounding surfaces using a very fine emergy disc and polish the whole area with an abrasive cleaner so that it blends in. Small chips and scratches of this type can be left in most cases without fear of the damage getting worse because the gel coat still provides a seal against water getting into the laminate. The touching up treatment suggested is only really necessary if you are concerned about the cosmetic appearance of your boat.

More serious are chips and scratches which extend into the laminate. These can usually be identified as a white surface under the gel coat with a fibrous texture. If the damage is minor with only the gel coat having been removed, then follow the same procedure as described above, but make sure that you grind back the gel coat to a point where there is positive adhesion between the gel coat and the laminate underneath. This can be checked by picking at the bond between the gel coat and the laminate with the sharp point of a knife. If the gel coat can be lifted, then you will have to grind back a bit further until you find a strong bond. Make sure that the exposed laminate is completely dry; this can be helped by directing a hair dryer or similar hot air blower on to the laminate although be careful not to raise the temperature too high. Once the area is thoroughly dry you then paint the gel coat over the exposed laminate and build it up to a level which matches the surrounding gel coat before grinding it down and polishing as explained previously.

If the damage actually extends into the laminate, then it may require more extensive treatment. Firstly put a straight edge across the damaged

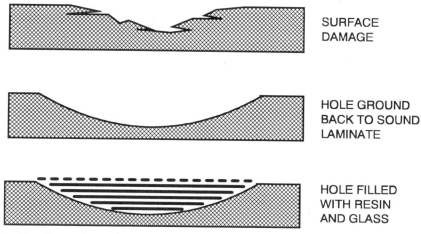

SURFACE
DAMAGE

HOLE GROUND
BACK TO SOUND
LAMINATE

HOLE FILLED
WITH RESIN
AND GLASS

Repairing damage in the GRP hull of a RIB. When the damage does not extend right through the laminate, it is ground out to sound material and then filled with layers of fresh laminate and finished off with matching gel coat.

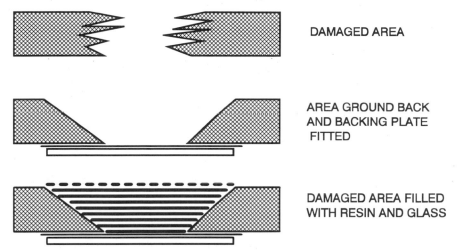

DAMAGED AREA

AREA GROUND BACK
AND BACKING PLATE
FITTED

DAMAGED AREA FILLED
WITH RESIN AND GLASS

When the hole extends right through the laminate the procedure is similar to that shown opposite except that a backing plate is needed to support the fresh laminate.

area, making sure that it is level with the clean gel coat on either side, and check the depth of the damaged area. If this is relatively shallow, perhaps just a millimetre or two, then you can probably get away with filling the damaged area with gel coat without any significant loss of strength. However, if there is any doubt, then you will need to grind out the whole of the damaged area, including any areas of delamination between the layers of the laminate, back to a clean, fresh surface. Now you can lay up new laminate inside the ground out area. It is best to use epoxy resins for this lay up because they are stronger than the normal vinyl resins commonly used in the original laminate. After building up the laminate in this way you may need to grind down the surface after it has cured, so that you can lay up the gel coat on top of the laminate and complete the repair.

More extensive damage to the GRP hull of a rigid inflatable can be repaired by an owner who is prepared to tackle the job methodically. If damage has lead to a complete puncture of the hull, then ideally you want access to both the inside and outside to produce an effective repair. The technique is to cut away all the loose pieces of fibreglass right back to sound laminate and then grind the edges on both sides down to a fine taper. Laminate can then be applied to both sides of the hole, gradually building up the layers, preferably using epoxy resins. On the inside, a generous overlap of material will help to provide continuity and allow you to build up the outside layer to conform with the existing shape in a repair which will be as strong as the original laminate. You will need some sort of backing to provide support for the laminate as you lay it up and the best material to use is a piece of formica or similar rigid plastic sheeting which can be attached to the outside of the hull whilst you lay up the inside. This will give a smooth contour to the new laminate and it is then relatively simple to grind down the surface and apply gel coat, after the laminate is cured, to complete the repair work.

Without access to the inside, then your repair job can be a bit more tricky and you have to resort to other techniques. You prepare the damaged area in much the same way, grinding back to sound laminate but in this case the taper is from the outside towards the inside in a gentle curve. You still need something to support the laminate whilst it is being built up and one method is to again use a piece of formica for the job. Because the hole is rarely regular in shape it will inevitably be longer one way than the other, so cut the piece of formica so that it will pass through the hole in its longest direction and you can then turn it round so that it covers the whole area of the hole once it is in position. To hold it in position, a temporary wooden handle can be attached to the formica which extends through the hole you are trying to repair. A few dabs of suitable adhesive can be used to hold the formica in place against the inside of the hull and then you have a base against which to carry out the repair work. Of course you will have to unscrew the handle before you start the repair work and then lay up the laminate against the formica, gradually extending it over the gently tapered existing laminate. A final coat or two of gel coat, which is then ground down and polished, completes the repair.

This technique shows the sort of ingenuity that is necessary when making repairs to GRP components. With most laying up or patch attachments you need a hard surface against which to roll out the laminate or the fabric and once you have devised a way of doing this then you have probably cracked the technique of repair work. If you are in any doubts about how a particular technique is going to work, try to practice on a part which is not critical or even on a separate piece of boat or structure before trying it for real.

Repairing the tubes

As far as the air tubes and fabrics of the boats are concerned, you first need to carefully inspect the surfaces looking for areas where the outer proofing of the fabric has been worn away, where taping and seals may

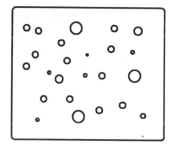
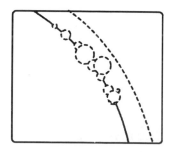

SMALL BUBBLES
INDICATE POROSITY

BUBBLES CONCENTRATED
ALONG A LEAKING SEAM

When a tube is tested for leaks, small bubbles appearing over the fabric surface away from seams indicates porosity. The second diagram shows bubbles appearing from a leak in a seam.

have lifted, and any other evidence of damage or decay, especially in the more inaccessible areas. Also check such items as handholds, fender strips, bow rings and transoms. You should not be able to lift any of the joints, seams or patches when you pick at the edge with your fingernail. If you do find any areas where there is lifting or wear and tear, then mark these with a ball point pen or magic marker to ensure that they receive further attention.

You will probably be aware of whether or not the boat is leaking air during your regular use of the boat, but now is a good time to check out the air holding qualities of the tubes by inflating them hard and painting them all over with a soft brush dipped in a foamy detergent solution. As we have already mentioned, if there are any air leaks they will soon become evident because bubbles will form. Modern fabrics mostly have excellent air-holding characteristics and you shouldn't have any problems but older fabrics, particularly those where the rubber was knifed rather than calendared on to the base fabric, do sometimes suffer from porosity which will be evident as a series of pin prick leaks over an area of the surface. Other leaks will be obvious as a series of bubbles forming in a particular spot or perhaps along the edge of a seam. These should all be marked with a ball point pen which will be visible once the tube dries off. Whilst checking for fabric leaks, also paint the detergent over and around the air valves to check these for airtightness.

Now you have the marked areas which need attention around the boat you can make a start on the repairs. If the seam edges have lifted, then you will need to dry the affected areas thoroughly; again a hair dryer can be good for this. Separate the affected areas as far as possible, which means opening up a seam until you come to sound adhesive. It is possible to open up a seam or an attachment flange further by careful application of hot air from a hair drier into the gap using a fine nozzle. The heat will soften the adhesive and allow you to peel it back gently; in this way you can be sure that you have got back to a sound bond before starting the repair. Now sandpaper the exposed surfaces between the two edges of the seam, or the patch and the air tube in the case of an attachment, so that you have a good key for the adhesive. Whilst holding the surfaces apart, firstly clean them with Toluene, Acetone or a cleaning liquid supplied by adhesive manufacturers, then apply the adhesive, making sure that both surfaces are completely covered in a thin layer. Let this first coat dry for about 15 minutes and then apply a second coat of adhesive. Once this is tacky, after about 10 minutes, you can press the two surfaces together, starting from the back of the seam and working towards the edge to exclude all the air, using as much pressure as possible. It may be better to do this work with the tube deflated so that you can use a small roller to remove any air from the gap, and this will also allow you to apply good pressure to the two surfaces so that they bond properly. After a few minutes you can then clean up any excess adhesive with one of the solvents mentioned above. The adhesive will take around 48 hours to fully cure and you should then have a seam or attachment which is ready for another season's use.

These maintenance type of repairs are quite straightforward providing you can get reasonable access to the area. They are not generally critical repairs compared with those which involve a serious air leak or damage to the fabric. These can be divided into five different types all demanding a different approach:

- The small repair which may be anything from a pin prick to a tear 5 cm long.
- A tear up to around 25 cm in length, provided that it doesn't go through any seam in the air tube, or cover more than one compartment in the air tube.
- The major repair to extensive damage to the air tube which may require major surgery.
- Repair to damage on the fabric floor of an inflatable where you can get to both sides with relative ease.
- Repairs due to wear and tear causing chafe of the fabric.

The first of these is relatively straightforward and can usually be repaired with a single patch on the outside of the tube. The technique used is to cut a patch with rounded corners from material similar to that from which the tube is made. This can usually be obtained from the manufacturer of the boat or a service and repair agent. If the fabric has neoprene on one side and Hypalon on the other, make sure that you use the material the same way round as the way it is used in the boat, which normally means having the Hypalon on the outside. Cut the patch to extend 5 cm clear of the tear or puncture, so that you have a good overlap, place the patch on the tube and mark round its edge. Prepare both the patch and the tube by lightly sanding the surface. You can use an electric sander for this job provided you use it with care and don't take off too much of the rubber. It is vital that you achieve a fresh, clean surface otherwise the adhesive will not do its job properly. Once you have cleaned the rubber don't touch it with your fingers because you will transmit grease to the surface, and the

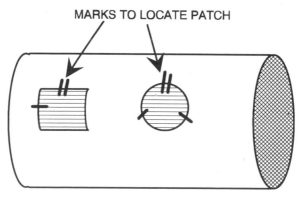

MARKS TO LOCATE PATCH

Small patches on the inflatable tube. The marks are made on both the tube and patch when dry to help line up the patches when the adhesive is applied.

adhesive won't stick in these areas. Use a solvent to clean the sanded area thoroughly. After this you may need to re-mark the position of the patch on the air tube if the original markings have been removed; you use this mark as a guide as you apply a thin, even coat of adhesive to both the patch and the tube, allowing a small overlap on the tube. Again, allow the adhesive to dry before applying a second coat. Once this has become tacky, you can then position the patch on the tube using the marked lines as a guide. When you do this make sure the tube is lying deflated on a flat hard surface and apply the patch with a rolling motion, one side first and gradually smoothing it across the whole area so that air is forced out and doesn't become trapped as a bubble. You only have one chance to get the patch in the right place because bonding of the adhesive is instantaneous. If you do get it wrong, careful application of heat from a hair dryer will help to release the bond, but you will probably have to apply another coat of adhesive and go through the process again. Once the patch has been applied to the air tube, flatten the surface with a small hard roller starting at the centre and working outwards. A roller comprised of several discs is better than a solid roller. The aim of rolling the patch is both to improve the bond between the two components and also to help roll out any air bubbles from the adhesive area which may have become trapped. Pay particular attention to the bonding around the edge of the patch and when the patch looks firm and secure you can then clean it up with the solvent that you used before. Allow the patch to cure for at least 12 hours before inflating the tube – longer if you possibly can.

For large tears in the inflatable tube then an inside patch is necessary to give the repair adequate strength. It may sound impossible to put a patch on the inside of a tube, but it can be done with a bit of careful planning. First widen the hole to around 10 cm, if it is not already this size, so that you can get your hand inside. Now cut a patch which has an overlap of at least 5 cm and follow the same procedure as before, cleaning up the tube surfaces inside the tube and on the patch, buffing them with sand paper to get a fresh clean surface and finally cleaning them with a solvent. Now

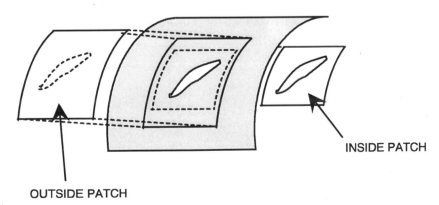

INSIDE PATCH

OUTSIDE PATCH

Applying patches to a large hole or tear. The inside patch is applied first to create the seal and then the outside patch to finish off the job and restore the fabric strength.

you apply adhesive to both the inside areas of the air tube and to the surface of the patch, let them become tacky as previously described, and then apply a second coat. Now you come to the tricky part where you have to get this patch inside the air tube. The best thing is to try a dummy run first without the adhesive so that you know the sort of procedure to adopt and then slide the patch into the air tube, pressing the tube firmly down on top of it. It sounds easy but is quite a tricky manoeuvre because as soon as any two layers of adhesive touch, they will want to stay together, and you can end up with a sticky mess unless you plan the operation carefully. You can use thin polythene sheet to cover the adhesive so that it won't stick, and then peel it off before making the final attachment, but try one side of the tear first and then the other so that you can line them up evenly. Once in position, rub the air tube down firmly with the roller to exclude any air bubbles, leave for 12 hours or so and then try inflating the tube to a pressure of not more than 2 psi to ensure that you have a proper bond and air tightness. Now you can tackle the outside of the tube, the method here follows the same procedure as for a small tear except that you will be dealing with a larger patch which will need more careful handling but again should be applied at one end first and then gradually rolled into position along the length of the tear.

Some people recommend that, with a longer tear, it is stitched with a needle and thread to restore some of the strength of the fabric and to hold the two sides of the tear in position whilst a repair is made. Against this has to be argued that it is impossible to put on an inside patch if you adopt this technique and secondly it is almost impossible to get an even,

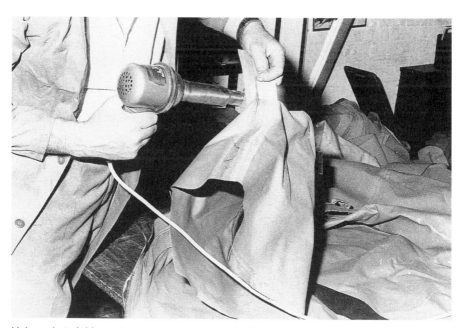

Using a hot air blower to open up seams on a badly damaged inflatable.

professional-looking repair because the stitching will almost invariably show through the outside patch. With good gluing techniques and working in the right conditions this stitching should not be necessary and it is important to fix on an effective inside patch because you will then have a double seal against future air leakage from this potentially weak point.

Repairs to extensive damage are best left to service agents and boatyards to carry out. They have the experience and expertise to do this sort of repair properly and it does require a lot of planning and patience if you are going to get the job right. However it is not impossible for the amateur to do this sort of repair work, but it will often mean opening up the seams of an air tube to get access, and so you need to look carefully at how the boat is constructed originally and plan your tactics accordingly. It is not easy to give precise rules for these extensive repair jobs because each one may need a different approach. Opening up the air tubes can be done with the hot air blower and careful work with a knife-like tool to gradually peel the seams apart. If the seams are taped you need to take the tape off first and then tackle the seam itself, but once opened up, repairing the original damage can be relatively straightforward because you now have access to both sides of the tube. Bringing the tube back together can be a real problem but if you work it out carefully beforehand and follow a logical sequence of work, you should have a boat which is as good as new at the end of the job. The secret of this type of more extensive repair is careful planning; always try each operation as a dry run before you carry it out with the adhesive in place.

Probably the most difficult repair of this type is one where the tear extends over a seam. Any patch you apply over the seam will tend to leak because of the small step between one side of the seam and the other due to the thickness of the material. It is almost impossible to get an effective repair without carefully tapering the edge of the fabric so that there is a smooth transition from one layer of fabric to the next. Simply trusting to the adhesive to fill this gap will rarely work effectively. Probably the worst damage of all to repair is one where it goes through the bulkhead dividing two compartments. This really is a job for the professionals, and even they can find it hard to get an effective repair.

Among the easiest types of repair, for the owner to carry out, is one in the floor fabric of an inflatable boat. Here you have full access to both sides of the fabric and the patching material should be applied to both sides so as to restore full strength to the original fabric. The techniques are similar to any other repair work for this type of patch. Any patch on the surface of the inflatable tube or in the floor which comes into contact with the water, should be taped along the edges with thin neoprene or Hypalon impregnated tape. This tape is much thinner than the normal tube fabric so it provides less resistance to the water flow and is less likely to peel off under pressure.

Finally in our round up of repair techniques, the alternative type of repair which an owner might be faced with is where chafe has worn away the surface rubber or there is porosity over an area of the inflatable tube.

The basic technique is very similar to that already described, but because the size of the patch is likely to be larger than with most repair jobs you need to pay careful attention to the application of the patch, applying it down one side first and then carefully rolling it down over the tear pressing it as you do so to exclude any air bubbles until you reach the other side. It is much easier to get rid of air bubbles during the process of applying the patch than it is after it is attached and a job of this type should be done by two people: one to do the rolling and one to hold the patch so that it can be applied in a controlled manner. Indeed, with most repairs except the smallest, two people can do the job much better than one, and this co-ordinated approach will produce much better results.

The inflation valves found in inflatable boats are generally very reliable and if replacements are required then it is generally only the insert which needs replacing which is a straightforward job. Should the whole valve need replacing, then this job can be done by the owner but it does mean opening up one of the seams of the air tube to get access to the inside. You will need to use a hot air blower to remove the existing valve before gluing the new valve in position. After that it is a question of following the techniques already described to seal up the air tube again.

Adhesives

Adhesives come in two types: one-part and two-part. Single part adhesives are those normally supplied with a boat's repair kit and are certainly much easier to use if you have to make emergency repairs when away from facilities. The one-part adhesive remaining in the tube or tin can be used again, although it will deteriorate more quickly once the container has been opened. With a two-part adhesive, once the two parts are mixed then you have probably about one hour before the mixture goes off and becomes unusable. However the two-part adhesive does give a far superior bond which is why the manufacturers of inflatable boats always use it. These adhesives, of which Boscoprene 2404 is one of the most popular, do have quite critical operating requirements. For the 2404 the manufacturers quote a pot life of 6 to 8 hours in a closed container once mixed, and a shelf life of 9 months from the date of manufacture. The curing time is 48 hours although the bond strength continues to increase up to a maximum of 7 days. The curing rate can be accelerated by heating to not more than 70°C. The solvents used in these adhesives are similar to those used for cleaning the rubber fabrics and are usually a mixture of Toluene and Acetone. Bostik supplies its own specially developed cleaner/thinner for use with the adhesives, but the standard Toluene or Acetone solvent will do the job equally well. When using either solvents or adhesives, bear in mind that they are toxic and highly inflammable so that you need special care when using them in an enclosed space. Ideally, all repair work using adhesives should be done under controlled conditions with a temperature of at least 60°F, and with low humidity. In particular, high humidity is not conducive to effective repair work which is one of the reasons why repairs done outside are often much less effective than might be expected. If you have to carry out emergency repairs in poor conditions, especially damp, then try and create a mini-environment around the repair area which can be kept warm and dry for at least the critical two hours of the initial curing. For winter repair and maintenance work, a heated garage will usually provide adequate conditions for effective repair work but like everything else relating to the construction and repair of inflatables the conditions and the planning of the job are the main ingredients of success. A piece of boat fabric will look quite harmless after it has been cut and positioned unglued on the boat but that same piece of fabric will appear to have a mind of its own and want to curl up and stick to anything which comes near it once you have applied the adhesive. Simple techniques such as taping the patch to a beer can, or other cylindrical object, before you apply the adhesive means that you can keep the patch under control, and simply roll it into position. The same problems can occur when applying tape to a seam; a lightweight tape with adhesive on it will be extremely difficult to handle. Wrapping the tape around a can or similar object will help to control it as you apply it to the tube. With longer pieces of tape you can put polythene between the layers to stop them sticking together and in this way application can become a simple two-handed job and not a nightmare tangle of sticky tape.

CHAPTER 11

SPORTS AND ADVENTURE

The very nature of inflatables means that they can often reach inaccessible places, making them ideal for exploration. These boats are generally soundly built and seaworthy, safe when handled correctly, and yet they combine these features with the ability to travel at high speed in close contact with the water, setting the scene for adventure and fun. The fact that these boats are used by a wide variety of expeditions, in remote parts of the world, demonstrates their capabilities and for the leisure user, when used intelligently, inflatable and RIBs can open the door to a variety of adventurous possibilities.

Exploration by inflatable RIBs

Most people view inflatables and RIBs as boats for short trips, but they also offer the prospect of long distance cruising. The shallow draft of these boats makes it possible to operate close-in to rocks, opening up a whole new dimension of coastal cruising where you can get a viewpoint which is seldom available to cruising yachts and powerboats. With inflatables it is possible to explore the coastline, landing on remote beaches and generally seeing areas which, in most circumstances, remain inaccessible. This sort of cruising gives the opportunity to view wildlife which may not normally be seen.

There can be risks in this type of long distance cruising and there are certain precautions which are necessary in the interests of safety. Ideally, boats should be twin engined so that an engine failure does not immediately create a serious problem, but an equally safe approach is to cruise in company so that there are two or more boats ready to help if anyone gets into difficulties. However, it is no good just thinking that cruising in company solves the problems. Careful planning and trials are necessary to establish the right level of safety. You must make sure that all the boats involved are able to tow each other over considerable distances should the necessity arise. If you have some idea of the problems which could be involved in a long distance tow then you will be able to organise your trip accordingly and have contingency plans ready should things start to go wrong. One advantage of inflatables is that you have access to virtually every harbour, and if necessary, almost any beach if problems arise. If you are planning a cruise with a long, open water passage make sure you are well equipped to cope with emergencies by carrying suitable spares; tools, extra fuel, a VHF radio and survival gear.

Whilst the portable nature of inflatables gives them a special niche in the field of exploration, the rough and often bumpy ride of these boats does tend to render them unsuitable for cruising over longer distances. Bombard made an Atlantic crossing in an inflatable boat, but he was simply drifting and trying to prove survival techniques. It is the rigid inflatable which has really opened the door to long distance cruising and in Britain the Rigid Inflatable Exploration Club (RIBEX) specialises in planning and executing cruises to otherwise inaccessible islands or over long open stretches of water. RIBEX is very stringent about safety procedures on these voyages which have reached as far as the island of St Kilda in the Atlantic Ocean and up to the Faroe Islands as well as including less demanding trips to the Fastnet Rock and across the English Channel. These voyages may be a tough test of both boat and crew, but the harsh environment also provides a good testing ground for electronic navigation equipment.

Preparation for cruising

Apart from the safety of the boats for long distance cruising, the comfort of the crew is of vital importance. In either an inflatable or a RIB you are very exposed to the elements and if you plan to be at sea for several hours, good personal protection is essential. The risks of exposure in these conditions can be very real and you also have to be prepared for changes in the weather conditions on route which may prolong the voyage. The dry suit with layers of warm clothing underneath, is probably one of the best items of clothing for this type of cruising, but head and hand protection is equally important.

FUEL STOWAGE

Carrying sufficient fuel is also a problem on these long voyages and when working out fuel requirements you have to bear in mind that a twin engined boat operating on just one engine may burn considerably more fuel per mile than when the boat is running at speed on twin engines. Running out of fuel at sea is one of the biggest embarrassments you can endure, and careful calculations backed up by trial runs are necessary to establish that there is adequate fuel on board to cope with all the different situations which might arise. Carrying this extra fuel in addition to the normal tanks can be quite a problem – probably the best solution is to use the flexible type of fuel tank which tends to be easier to stow than rigid tanks. (See photo on page 47.)

However, make sure that any fuel stored in this way on deck is properly stowed and that the tanks cannot be damaged by sharp fixtures on the boat. Think carefully about how the fuel is to be transferred from these tanks (either into the main tanks or directly to the engine via a flexible fuel line) because what looks like an easy operation when you are in port, can be quite difficult to carry out on a boat tossing around at sea. Always use the fuel in the portable tanks first, because it will be more vulnerable to damage or contamination, and keep the fuel in the main tanks for the final part of the voyage.

NAVIGATION AND WEATHER

Electronic navigation, using fully waterproof instruments, can be a great boon on this type of long distance cruising; it gives you great confidence to know exactly where you are and where you are going. It is essential that you back up these instruments with charts, which have to be carried in waterproof cases if they are going to survive in the damp environment. Careful navigation pre-planning is a vital aspect of these voyages, and the charts need to be carefully marked with all the proposed courses as well as all the possible options which are open to you to cope with emergencies or with changing weather conditions. When planning navigation on these routes, there will be certain points of the voyage where decisions have to be made about whether to continue or whether to divert because of changed conditions, and these need to be clearly marked on the chart.

You will also need to take into account the wide variety of weather possibilities which you can encounter, and be prepared for sudden changes. Running into fog could add a whole new dimension to your navigation requirements and you need to plan carefully how and when you are going to make landfalls if the visibility is poor and think about all the options available to you. With long distance cruising in rigid inflatables, planning is not only the key to success, for many people this aspect is half the fun of making the voyage.

Camping Nautique

Cruising in inflatables and RIBs does not have to be all heroics and hardship, it can be carried out in a much more leisurely fashion. Cruising along a coastline with the option of landing on remote beaches or visiting bustling harbours can be a very attractive and interesting cruising option. The French have an expression for this, *camping nautique*, which is a cruising technique which involves taking all your camping equipment with you in the boat, so that when the time comes to stop for the night, you simply land on a suitable beach and set up camp. This type of cruising is best suited to warm, dry climates because, after a day in the boat, you really want the luxury of being able to dry out when you camp for the night. On inflatables or RIBs everything tends to get wet, and you can end up in quite a depressing situation if it is raining when you land on a beach to camp for the night and your wet gear just gets wetter!

Camping Nautique is a sport carried out widely in the Mediterranean where the conditions can often be perfect for this type of cruising. Certainly the remote beaches have an attraction – cooking over a fire made from driftwood, perhaps catching your own fish or launching the boat and going out to buy fish from a fishing boat out at sea, but largely enjoying the peace and quiet and remoteness of the surroundings. Whilst the idea of camping on remote beaches and being completely self-sufficient is one of the attractions of this type of cruising, it doesn't have to be all hardship, and the main criteria should be one of enjoyment. You can intersperse nights on remote beaches with harbour stop-overs, staying in a hotel where you can enjoy the luxury of a bath and a restaurant meal. There is no reason why you can't do this type of cruising with just a single boat, but again two or more boats cruising together does improve the safety margins and gives added manpower for handling boats on beaches.

Inflatables, rather than RIBs, are better for Camping Nautique. Inflatables are generally better for landing on a beach and lighter for carrying up to a safe point above high water. It is more difficult to pull rigid inflatables up a beach and the rigid hull is always vulnerable when you are nosing your way into a strange beach where there may be rocks that you can't see; charts rarely show up sufficient detail in the shallows. The inflatable boat is ideal for this type of operation; if you are unsure of what lies ahead, then you can always tilt the engine and paddle or row the boat into the shore. This is all part of the adventure of Camping Nautique and it is exciting to think that all the equipment for such an adventure can be packed into or on top of your car.

Sub-aqua diving

Inflatables and RIBs are the ideal small boat for inshore diving and they are popular with clubs and small groups throughout the world.

Inflatables are relatively cheap and easy to buy and maintain and they have the advantage that they can be light enough to be carried across beaches for launching. Most RIBs are too heavy to be carried, and require trailer launching but at sea they are fast, easy to helm and considered to be very stable and seaworthy. A 5 metre RIB is easily capable of carrying 6 divers and their equipment to a dive site.

A well-equipped diving RIB will have an anchor and rope, a separate throw-rope, a shot and line, a forward waterproof locker for flares, first aid and basic survival equipment and engine spares. On the console will be mounted a compass, Decca or GPS nav aids, echo sounder and VHF radio. A stainless steel bottle rack will be bolted to the floor forward or aft of the console so that air bottles can be stored upright securely. An A-frame aft will provide a siting for navigation lights, the antenna for the nav aid and aerial for the radio. Many clubs regard a prop guard as an important accessory on a dive boat to prevent any possibility of injury to divers from the prop when they are being picked up.

Another type of equipment which is increasingly being carried by dive boats is an oxygen kit. The rapid administration of 100% oxygen by a qualified person has proved to be highly beneficial for victims of decompression sickness, burst lung and carbon monoxide poisoning, whilst waiting for evacuation to a recompression facility.

DIVING PROCEDURE

Once the dive site is reached, the diving pairs kit up, do their checks and are briefed by the dive marshal. They enter the water easily by a backward roll over the tube. It is usual for a diver-cox to remain in charge of the boat with his buddy to give cover while his companions dive. The blue and white A-flag is prominently flown to warn approaching vessels that there are divers down. When on drift dives, each pair of divers carry a reel and line with a surface marker buoy (SMB) attached so that the cox can easily keep track of his divers. On a wreck dive, SMBs are not used because of the problem of entanglement with other divers' lines or the wreck itself. Instead, each pair carry a reel and line with a deflated delayed SMB attached. At the end of the dive, this is filled with air, either from its own separate supply or from the diver's own breathing set. This is released from depth and the cox is then aware that the divers are making their ascent.

Once the pair of divers have surfaced, they signal to the boat and the cox drives slowly towards them from downwind, putting the engine out of gear as he approaches to pick them up. When they are alongside they can hold on to the grablines or clip on while they take it in turn to dekit. The weight belt is handed into the boat followed by the aqualung set, once any direct feed hoses have been disconnected. Having removed the heaviest equipment, most divers then find it easy to enter the boat by finning hard and bearing down on the grablines to propel themselves over the tubes. It is helpful if a buddy on the boat removes the diver's fins before

A diver examines his find: a much prized porthole from a wreck. The rack safely holds 10 air bottles while the well-equipped console meets every need: compass sounder, electronic nav-aid, VHF radio, horn, fire extinguisher and emergency engine cut-out with lanyard. *Photo: Chinook.*

Above: This 6.5 metre RIB makes an ideal dive boat. Spacious enough for 6 divers, cox and equipment, its 145 hp petrol sterndrive engine makes light work of its load and is capable of planing at 30 knots. *Photo: Chinook*.

he swings his legs round into the boat. If the design and size of the boat makes it especially high out of the water, it is possible to climb up over the transom once the engine has been turned off. An important point in any diving operation is to ensure that the boat is always manned by a competent helmsman who is experienced enough to cope with any situation and be licenced to use the VHF radio to summon help should a diving emergency arise.

Water skiing

There is a tendency to associate water skiing with the glamour of gleaming sports boats. The polished finish of these stylish boats tends to go with the image of water skiing, yet inflatables and RIBs can provide very effective water ski tow boats. Even a boat only three or four metres long can be used for water skiing, provided that there is adequate engine power. Whilst the skiing may not be very exciting with this type of boat, it can provide a cheap and viable means of having fun on the water. An engine of 20 or 30 hp may be all that is necessary to get a skier up behind a small inflatable, but for more serious skiers an engine in the 50–70 hp range would be better.

Towing a skier behind an inflatable can make the driving very sensitive. Because the boat has a flat bottom, it has little bite on the water and so the actions of the skier behind, swinging from side to side, can in turn start to swing the tow boat unless the swings are corrected in the steering. Turns do need to be executed with a degree of care if you want to keep the skier up on his skis, so turning should be done gently without any sudden movements, but then that rule applies to all water skiing, not just with

Water skiing with an inflatable requires extra skill from the helmsman to prevent the skier from swinging the flat-bottomed craft round, especially on turns. *Photo: Mercury Marine.*

inflatables. However, the inflatable will tend to drift sideways on the turn and you will feel the need to put the helm over more to achieve the turn you want, with the result that you will lose forward momentum and skate sideways even more unless you keep a careful eye on the speed of the boat.

With a rigid inflatable you have none of these problems, because, to all intents and purposes, it behaves just like an ordinary sports boat and most RIBs are well equipped for water skiing. With a rigid inflatable, you also have the advantage that you can fit a proper towing post into the boat, perhaps a third of the way forward from the transom giving you better steering control which will make the ride better for the skier. On an inflatable, it is not practical to fit a towing post inside the boat; the normal solution is to fit a bridle to the transom which would take the tow line clear of the engine, and then have the single line extending to the skier from a point a metre or so behind the engine.

As with diving, inflatables and RIBs make recovery from the water a simple and easy operation. The low freeboard helps a great deal and the cushion effect of the air tube reduces the risks of injury when coming alongside. Because the person being recovered from the water is active, then the approach should normally be from down wind coming up into the wind. Keep the skier in the water as far away from the propellers as possible and stop the engines immediately contact has been made. When towing a skier, always be aware of the tow line and its potential for getting caught in the propellers, so once your skier is down recover the tow line before attempting any further manoeuvres to retrieve the person in the water. Stowing water skis inside the boat can be a problem; the best solution is to have rubber shock cords alongside the air tubes or on the deck to prevent the skis from sliding around the boat and causing damage when running to and from harbour.

Racing inflatables and RIBs

Racing with inflatables and RIBs has become a specialised sport and certainly in the inflatable market it has led to the development of many specialised types specifically designed to maximise speed. This is an interesting area of inflatable boat development although sadly, like many forms of racing, modifications have now outstripped every day inflatable boating and so the lessons being learned from racing are not necessarily relevant to inflatable boats in general. Racing categories tend to be limited by engine power and in order to increase speed, the boats need to be as light and efficient as possible. Light weight means a minimal type of boat whilst efficiency is generally improved by inflating the air tubes extremely hard, so that they form an effective planing surface. In these specialised dedicated racing boats, the ride is rough and hard and, as many of the races take place in open sea conditions, this is a tough sport aimed at the very fit and active person. It is generally a safe sport because speeds are not particularly high even though the ride is very exhilarating.

RIB racing is still a developing sport and the major race which is now becoming an annual event is the Round Scotland Race. This is in fact a series of daily races around the wild and often exposed Scottish coastline and this event certainly demonstrates the capabilities of the rigid inflatable to cope with difficult conditions. Again, these boats tend to be classed by

The control position of a racing rigid inflatable with specially designed sprung seats. RIB racing rules are kept very simple and mainly relate to safety, hence the mandatory crash helmets. *Photo: Mercury Marine.*

their engine capacity with diesel and petrol engined boats being separated into different categories. The safety rules are very strict and relate largely to common sense. Initially, this race attracted entries from standard commercial production boats, but it is now interesting to see that a trend is developing towards higher speeds and more specialised craft based around long slender lines. Specially sprung seats are fitted for the crew to reduce the bumping and jarring.

Inevitably, the urge to win leads to excessive design modification but it will be sad if RIB racing develops along the lines of inflatable boat racing, where only very specialised craft have a chance of success. It is very hard to write racing rules which make the competition equal for standard production boats, and whilst these more specialised racing RIBs are an interesting development, they will inevitably drift away from the main stream of rigid inflatable development although, hopefully, there will still be lessons to be learned from this work. In general, though, RIB racing has not yet become too ambitious and shorter handicap races are open to all competitors with a suitable boat so that they can race on fairly even terms. This type of racing remains one of the few areas where racing in production boats is still practical.

Adventure on inland waterways

Rivers and inland waterways can provide fascinating cruising grounds for both inflatables and RIBs and you can tackle these at any level at which you feel competent. The inflatable boat is ideal for cruising on rivers and waterways, particularly with its ability to go alongside or land virtually anywhere. But, at its more extreme levels, inflatable boats are used for river running or white water rafting as it is sometimes called - travelling down untamed rivers and negotiating rapids in a wild and seemingly uncontrolled ride. The boats used for this are of the fully inflatable type, specially designed and built for the job and controlled by oars or paddles. These oars or paddles are not really for propulsion but largely for steering, trying to keep the boat pointing in the right direction. The skill of this sport is in reading the river ahead to find the safest route, and then attempting to steer the boat into the right part of the river to follow the desired course. There are risks in this sport and certainly participants need to be carefully briefed and equipped for falling overboard into the white water. Experience has shown that seemingly impossible river conditions can be negotiated by boats in this way.

Whilst the completely inflatable boat appears to be the ideal type of craft for this type of white water rafting, these boats also have the benefit of being portable. They can be deflated, folded up completely and taken back to the starting point again. Indeed, perhaps the major snag with this sport is that the passage down a river is a one way trip and at the end of the day you need to transport the boat back to the starting point again. With any kind of river exploration you need back up transportation between stopping places.

There are also inflatable kayaks and other small craft which can be used for individual river descents but, in the interests of safety, it is sensible to operate at least in pairs. As regards equipment for these boats, the main requirement, apart from the oars and paddles, are long lengths of rope which allow the boats to be lowered down the more extreme sections of rivers and can also be used to haul the boats across from one side of the

An inflatable, which can be easily transported by land, makes an ideal boat for exploring unusual waters such as this underground cave system. *Photo: Avon Inflatables.*

river to another, or simply for mooring. Fully waterproof bags for personal equipment and camping gear are also a requirement, but much depends on whether you are just doing short trips down a river or planning long expeditions and what sort of back up and facilities are available on the shore. Crash helmets and lifejackets are mandatory equipment to reduce injuries.

Passports to adventure

You will see from this chapter that there is a wide range of areas where inflatables and RIBs can be used for exploration and sport. There is no doubt that the inflatable and the RIB have opened up many possibilities in the marine world which were not previously attainable or practical. The capabilities of the inflatable to cope with a wide variety of difficult or even extreme conditions has opened up, many routes to adventure, but you need to bear in mind, when embarking on these sports, that even the best boats can let you down at times, and so safety precautions are very necessary. Planning and preparation are the main essentials so that you anticipate just what you are going into and what the risks are. With inflatables and rigid RIBs the margins between success and failure can be quite small at times and you need to have a strong awareness of the dangers, but then so often it is the challenge of the risks and your ability to cope with them which make the sport exciting.

CHAPTER 12

PROFESSIONAL USE OF INFLATABLES

Up until the 1950s inflatables had been considered very much a plaything, a toy for calm waters and fun. The inflatable liferaft was probably the first serious use of inflatable boats by professionals. The French Lifeboat Society introduced inflatable rescue boats along many areas of the coast of France in the late 1950s and Britain followed suit. At that stage materials and construction methods still left something to be desired and the advantages of using an inflatable had to be balanced against the high maintenance requirements and the lack of reliability. Improved construction and materials together with more reliable outboards helped to make a convincing case for these versatile rescue boats. Within a matter of just a year or two of their introduction, these inshore lifeboats were rescuing just as many people as the all weather, all-year-round conventional lifeboats. Speed was becoming a vital factor in rescue work with the change in pattern of casualties and it was this which convinced rescue authorities that there was a need for fast inflatable inshore lifeboats.

Rescue work

Today, inflatables are widely used for rescue, both by the RNLI and many other authorities who are involved with rescue work at sea and in lakes and rivers. The inflatable still reigns supreme for launch and recovery because of the ease at which it can be handled over beaches and in difficult launching situations. It is relatively light in weight, easy to handle, and with modern materials and engines, is both reliable and requires little maintenance.

Many of these same qualities have been used to develop a rescue boat for carrying on board ships. This is now a requirement for many large types of ships, but also for smaller craft such as tugs and fishing boats where the inflatable lifeboat is used in conjunction with liferafts as the main means of evacuation. These rescue/lifeboats carried on board ships are inherently the same basic design as those used for rescue work and leisure use. The main difference is in the equipment they are required to carry to ensure safe evacuation and survival. The reliability of modern outboard motors mean that they are an acceptable form of propulsion for both regulation lifeboats and rescue boats. The authorities consider that only low speed is necessary so outboard motors of probably no more than 10 hp are used on these boats; however, the use of low power will make the craft more prone to capsize in rough seas, a fact that the authorities should take into account when assessing the capabilities of modern inflatables.

Inflatables for military and commercial use

Inflatables are also carried on board many military and paramilitary craft for boarding, evacuation, and as general workboats. Although the inflatable is being replaced by the RIB for many of these applications, it is still attractive for many roles because of easy stowage, relatively light weight and portability. Inflatables are widely used as portable assault or boarding boats by the military, and various types have been developed where the floorboards are incorporated as an integral part of the design, so that simply by the inflation process, the whole boat is assembled and ready for use. Avon has developed a 4 metre inflatable of this type which incorporates gas cylinder inflation so that the boat can be ready for use within 10 or 15 seconds. This type of boat is used on board submarines and other small military craft, but it can also be used for an air drop, with the engine already mounted, so that on inflation the boat is virtually ready for immediate use. In the military field, the cost tends to be secondary to the requirement so that these specialised boats are usually very expensive. This is why many of these developments have not been adopted by the leisure or more general professional market where cost tends to be a much more significant factor.

Inflatables being used for vehicle transportation on the Camel Trophy in Guyana. *Photo: Avon Inflatables.*

There have been other specialised developments of inflatable boats for particular requirements and one is in the form of an oil barge for holding oil recovered from oil pollution recovery operations. The main reason for using inflatable components is that simply by applying an air line to the inflation valves, the barge can be inflated very quickly and is then ready for use and when not required it takes up the minimum of storage space. These barges have been developed in sizes which can hold up to 500 tonnes of oil and they can be towed at slow speed with this cargo on board. This type of development clearly demonstrates the versatility of using inflatable rather than conventional rigid craft.

RIBs for rescue

Inflatable craft such as these barges tend to have been relegated to more specialised applications with the advent of the rigid inflatable. There is no doubt that the RIB, since its original evolution back in the 1960s, has taken the workboat and military market by storm. There has been such a huge amount of development work that the rigid inflatable has been established as a viable and practical high speed small craft for many military and workboat applications. Originally developed for rescue work, this still remains one of the main areas of use with most lifeboat authorities around the world adopting the RIB in one form or another. Larger versions with enclosed wheelhouses have been designed as all-weather lifeboats by some authorities with the Dutch being notably forward in this type of development work. In larger sizes of 12–15 metres in length, the RIB combines good stability at low speeds with an integral fendering arrangement which can prove invaluable in lifeboat work. However, such is the conservatism in lifeboat development, that the wider acceptance of the rigid inflatable as an all-weather lifeboat will take some time. But this does seem to be an inevitable development and the pioneering work being undertaken by the Dutch lifeboat authorities is being watched very closely.

There are two approaches to the use of rigid inflatables in lifeboat work, one concept using the fully inflatable tube and in some cases taking this right round the hull to give added protection. The other uses the foam-filled tube which as we have seen in previous chapters, provides fendering but not the ability to deform under wave pressure.

Professional use of RIBs

Experience in using rigid inflatables for shore-based rescue work led to the adoption of the RIB as a rescue boat in North Sea oil operations. Major disasters on oil rigs and platforms in the North Sea pointed out the need for standby vessels which could be available for rescue and recovery duties in any emergency. In turn, these standby vessels which, at that time, were mainly converted trawlers, were required to have a rescue boat which could be launched to go to the aid of survivors in the water and this is where the rigid inflatable came in. The experience with the RNLI rescue

A rigid inflatable rescue boat, which incorporates a wheelhouse, used for North Sea Offshore oil operations. *Photo: Boston Putford.*

boats was the focus for this development and originally the Atlantic 21 was the yardstick for these offshore oil rescue boats. Since that time, a range of specialised designs have been developed and the emphasis now tends to be away from using outboard motors with a switch towards diesel engines combined with water jets for propulsion. The switch to diesel engines gives the rescue boats a compatible fuel with the mother ship and the use of water jets reduces the risk to survivors in the water or damage during launch and recovery. In general, these boats have performed well but there has been a steep learning curve, particularly for the launch and recovery. In many cases the different requirements for launching from a mother ship compared with launching from a shore have not been fully recognised and the use of self-righting equipment on these offshore oil rescue boats is probably an unnecessary refinement. Also many

of these latest generation of rescue boats have become very complex and sophisticated leading to maintenance problems in the offshore environment. The design and construction of these boats is now largely covered by strict rules and regulations which, in many cases, do not leave much latitude for innovation. However, the rules do allow the use of foam filled tubes and several operators have switched to this option on the misconceived basis that it will reduce maintenance and improve reliability without considering the effect of this switch on the seaworthiness of the boat.

The fact that the military, in their use of rigid inflatables, almost entirely use inflatable air tubes rather than the foam-filled type demonstrates that they at least recognise the virtues of using the air tube and the improvement it gives in the seaworthiness of the boats. Navies around the world now use RIBs almost without exception as sea and boarding boats, and

Coming alongside a mother ship. If both mother ship and inflatable maintain steering way the whole operation is a lot more controllable. *Photo: Carson Inflatables.*

they have proved versatile and practical in this application. Unfortunately the launch and recovery systems used for many of these military and off-shore oil industry craft, have not matched the developments in the boats themselves and so many are both crude and inefficient. It is probably fair to say that it is in this area of launch and recovery that the use of the rigid inflatable as a boarding and sea boat is being restricted and its full potential is not being realised.

New markets are constantly being developed for RIBs, partly as a result of new design concepts, but also as there is a wider recognition of the capabilities of the craft. A rigid inflatable pilot boat is now in operation and this 13 metre craft is proving very effective in service but once again there is a strong element of conservatism in this sector, because of the difficult operating conditions under which pilot boats often have to operate, so that this prototype development is being watched with a great deal of interest. There are many other areas in the harbour craft market where the RIB could be used but the potential is only slowly being recognised and, of course the higher costs of a rigid inflatable compared with more conventional craft tends to restrict its application.

The new generation of very high speed rigid inflatables is attracting attention from the military market as a fast patrol boat. Initial trials suggest that this type of RIB could be extremely effective on anti-smuggling patrol and similar operations where the boat operates as a stand-alone unit. The inflatable air tubes give a very low radar signature to the boat and they also allow it to operate safely and comfortably at low speeds in the loitering mode. Their effectiveness in this role is perhaps demonstrated by the fact that boat builders have received requests for this type of high speed RIB from the smugglers themselves. The advent of rigid inflatables with wheelhouses will extend their role even further. This ability to provide weather protection can be important on extended patrol duties.

Size for size, the RIB does tend to be more expensive than its rigid hulled counterpart and with cost becoming a sensitive issue as far as professional use is concerned, this may have a retarding factor on development. However, it is effectiveness which tends to be the important factor as far as professional workboat and military applications are concerned, and here the larger rigid inflatable is only starting to demonstrate its capabilities. When these are fully appreciated, particularly with the installation of twin diesels and water jet propulsion, there is the possibility that the rigid inflatable will take over a considerable proportion of the workboat market in the future. There seems to be no obvious limit to the size of rigid inflatable which could be built except that the air tube can only resist a certain amount of momentum so that it is likely to be the increased weight which would make the air tube impractical.

The tourist market is taking to both the inflatable and the RIB. Inflatables are used mainly for white water passenger trips down rivers while rigid inflatables are being used to take tourists in close to sights such as whales, cliffs or caves. There is much scope for development here and

Perhaps the ultimate rigid inflatable development is the whale-watching boat produced by Naiad in New Zealand. This sophisticated craft meets the requirements for commercial passenger carrying boats. *Photo: Naiad.*

the authorities have taken a fairly positive attitude to safety regulations for these boats. In Britain all workboats, including inflatables and RIBs, now come under a comprehensive set of safety rules and regulations. As many of these are based on the rescue boat standards, most boats with inflatable tubes can meet them easily. Rules and regulations do seem to be impinging on to the inflatable and rigid inflatable markets as far as professionals are concerned. This does tend to restrict development because there is no incentive to exceed the requirements but to balance this it does also bring respectability to the market for these boats.

CHAPTER 13

ALTERNATIVE CONCEPTS

Throughout this book so far the accent has been on what might be termed conventional designs of inflatable and RIB which tend to have a reasonably boat-like shape, with pointed bow and transom stern. However, there is quite a range of alternative concepts in both the inflatable and RIB market and these can offer practical solutions to the requirements of some operators and users.

Catamarans

One of the concepts, which logically extended into the inflatable market, was the catamaran. As far as rigid hulls are concerned, the catamaran is well proven and is the preferred design where very high speeds are sought, or where stability is required as in the sailing catamaran. For inflatables there is a lot of logic in the catamaran concept because it calls for two straight tubes which makes construction much simpler and potentially cheaper; but designers are then faced with the problem of linking these two tubes together. Inflatable components have not proved particularly satisfactory for this and inflatable cats have tended to end up with a rigid bow and transom with the tubes linking the two. This does not produce the most seaworthy boat shape but it does create a viable and practical alternative where seaworthiness is not the prime consideration. Some yacht tenders are built to this format and catamaran hulls are also used for many of the specialised designs used in inflatable racing. For racing, the reduced resistance of two long, narrow tubes can be less than that of a conventional inflatable and when the tubes are inflated very hard they create an efficient planing surface.

In the rigid inflatable market, twin hulls have been used for the rigid part of the catamaran hull rather than the air tubes, but they haven't been very successful. The reason is that the catamaran hull shape on its own has better stability than a monohull and so there is less need to put the inflatable tubes round the outside for stability. The wider beam of the catamaran does not lend itself comfortably to accepting the inflatable tubes because it produces a boat with a wider beam than is practical in relation to the length and it throws up the problem of what to do at the bow. A cross tube at the bow is the only logical solution, but this does not produce particularly good characteristics when operating in a following sea. In general, the use of catamaran hulls, despite their increased efficiency at higher speeds, has not proved either popular or successful in the rigid inflatable market. However, there is an acceptable compromise for particular applications. The solution is to use a trihedral type of hull which has a squared off bow installed in the form of a ramp. This converts the rigid inflatable, which has two straight sided tubes, into a landing craft type of craft and this concept, although it has reduced seaworthiness compared with a conventional RIB, certainly makes a very practical workboat, possibly even suitable for diving and rescue work. The ability to lower the ramp when landing on a beach makes it suitable for loading and discharging smaller items of cargo on remote beaches, whilst the same ramp could be used as a recovery point for survivors from the water, literally scooping them up over the bow. This could certainly be an acceptable solution when injured survivors are involved. The same design could also be suitable for diver deployment and recovery, particularly if a ladder is built into the bow ramp. This landing craft design may usefully meet certain practical requirements, but as with most modifications, a penalty has to be paid, and in this case it tends to be in the form of less effective handling in rough seas.

High-speed RIBs

Whilst inflatable boat racing has developed some interesting and novel designs for high speed, usually related to very high pressure tube inflation and narrowing planing surfaces, the more conventional rigid inflatable market is also moving into high performance. The demand for high speed RIBs comes from both racing and the military market. In the latter, where operators want to combine speed for pursuit with the ability to go alongside boats at sea without damage, the rigid inflatable provides an ideal solution. Even conventional RIB designs, using either large outboards or twin inboard diesels, can achieve top speeds of 50 or 60 knots. But one rigid inflatable built in Italy, probably the fastest built so far, has a top speed in the high 80 knot range.

In concept, this rigid inflatable appears remarkably conventional, although it has a higher length/beam ratio than is normal. It is based around a 12 metre GRP hull designed specifically for offshore powerboat racing which has a 24 degree deadrise and incorporates two steps into the hull. This highly successful, well-proven underwater hull shape, powered by twin 1000 hp diesel engines, was converted into a rigid inflatable by simply producing a new deck moulding, reducing the topsides on the hull moulding and adding the inflatable tube. The result is a boat which combines incredible seaworthiness and the ability to make excellent progress in rough seas combined with a very high top speed. This design is an extension of RIB development but approaches the problem from a different direction. Most fast rigid inflatables have been developed from smaller versions, whereas this FB Design RIB has been developed from a 100 knot racing boat which has then been modified and adapted for the rigid inflatable requirements, whilst still retaining most of the high performance characteristics. The four-man cockpit has been specially designed for high speed with deeply upholstered bolsters to support the crew and carefully placed controls which allow the boat to be handled very delicately even in adverse conditions. This boat is one of the first rigid inflatables to use surface-piercing propellers which are very efficient at high speeds. With this design, the hub of the propeller is on a level with the water line exiting the transom when the boat is travelling at high speed; only the bottom blades are working whilst the top blades operate in the air. The advantage is that only the propeller blades are in the water, so that drag from the propeller shaft and its supports is virtually eliminated.

Now that this design from Italy has shown the way, it is likely that high performance will be sought in the rigid inflatable market as military users become more aware of the characteristics and performance capabilities of these boats. Here is an excellent example of the way in which a RIB can combine the often conflicting requirements of good stability at low speed with high performance. As the boat comes off the plane, the air tubes enter the water and provide the additional stability whilst the tube also provides excellent fendering when going alongside other craft. Add to this the ability of the air tube to distort under wave impact at very high speed and it can be appreciated how this boat has better rough water performance than a conventional rigid hulled craft.

One possible type of development with this boat is to have an air manifold linked to the various compartments in the air tube and coupled to vacuum and pressure pumps on the engines. This will allow the pressure in the air tube to be varied when the boat was underway and in this way its condition response could be matched more closely to the required performance of the boat. This certainly increases the complexity of the boat, but when you are seeking the ultimate in performance this has to be accepted. Another adaptation on this particular boat is the incorporation of a bow ballast tank in the rigid part of the hull which can be filled from the engine cooling system and emptied via a dump valve. This tank adds weight to the bow of the boat which helps to prevent the bow flying skyward when operating at high speed in head seas.

Inflatables for sailing

In complete contrast, there are inflatables and RIBs which can be used for sailing. Sailing is generally restricted to the yacht tender type of inflatable boat where the addition of a mast, centreboard and rudder allows the boat to be used for fun sailing as well as a means of transport to and from the shore. Many people may think that this is trying to fit too much into the concept of the small inflatable boat, but in boats like the Tinker Tramp, the sailing requirements have been achieved without too much compromise and although you will never get the best performance out of such a rig, it is a viable alternative to the conventional dinghy hull.

The Tinker Tramp uses a centreboard which is rigged in a waterproof fabric slot on the centreline of the boat. Other sailing inflatables incorporate lee boards linked by a cross member across the inflatable tubes. The mast is usually mounted either on a cross-thwart or directly on to the rigid floorboards, whilst the rudder is mounted on the brackets at the stern. The rig for sailing inflatables is generally kept very simple, often with only a single sail. They also often have twin transoms, one at the stern and one at the bow which provides more space inside the boat. Sailing RIBs could also be particularly suitable for beginners with the additional buoyancy of the air tube providing extra stability when the vessel heels over with the wind but this approach has not been pursued so far.

River running

The sport of river running, letting the water flow take inflatable boats down wild and raging torrents, has led to the development of a specialised range of inflatables. The primary aim in the design of river running boats is to remove all the hard components such as transom and floor boards

A sailing inflatable. The Tinker Tramp is basically a yacht tender which can be adapted for sailing and as a rescue raft.

which could easily be damaged. The boats are built entirely of inflatable tubing, generally with a very heavy duty fabric floor. This allows the boat to survive impact with rocks and to adapt its shape, conforming to the flow of the rushing water. River running boats tend to be controlled either by people paddling, sitting astride the air tubes to get the necessary leverage, or alternatively by oars which are rigged in a frame inside the boat with the rower looking forward so that he can read the river and manoeuvre the boat accordingly. Good handholds are a vital part of any river running boat and so is some means of stowing your gear in watertight containers, because inevitably everything gets very wet and some form of dry stowage is essential. These boats often fill with water and drainage can be provided by using a form of double floor with holes around the edge which form a type of crude one way valve, allowing the water to drain out but not to flow in.

Flying RIBs

It seems that inflatables and RIBs are very versatile, but one of the most extreme ideas must be a flying RIB. The idea may sound far fetched but flying RIBs have actually been built and demonstrated in Italy, and for those seeking adventure and fun, these could have some appeal. Flying RIBs have been developed by combining microlight and rigid inflatable technology. Propulsion both in the water and in the air comes from an air-cooled engine driving an air propeller mounted on an A-frame bolted to the rigid part of the deck which also supports the wings. The pilot/driver is seated in the front of the boat, in front of the A-frame controlling the boat/aeroplane via an air rudder and by weight distribution. The whole rig has to be built as light as possible so that it can reach critical speed and take-off and the hull is very small to reduce weight so that on the water, these boats/aeroplanes are only viable for calm waters, especially as the wings have to be folded and stowed before making progress on water. The flying RIB becomes a bit impractical in terms of regular usage but is a great boat for fun in the right conditions. Different countries will have different requirements for a pilot's licence for such a flying inflatable and it is best to check this before investing in a rigid inflatable of this type.

If you want to fly but stay closer to the water, then an inflatable hovercraft might be the answer. This is really rigid inflatable rather than inflatable boat technology because with this type of craft, both the crew and the engine tend to be mounted on a rigid platform above the inflatable hull. The air chamber on which the boat rides is formed underneath the platform and hull within a skirt attached to the outer edge of the inflatable tube. Inflatable hovercraft of this type are very practical craft and the tube has particular benefit when going alongside. At slow speeds, hovercraft are not always the most controllable craft. Control is generally by weight distribution combined with using a rudder working in the slipstream of the air propeller. Driving and controlling hovercraft requires new skills because they are air rather than water borne craft and they will be much more affected

A flying rigid inflatable. This uses microlight technology and the air propeller provides propulsion in both water and in the air.

by the wind when riding 'on cushion' than a boat in the water. This means that they tend to skate sideways in a turn which has to be allowed for when manoeuvring. The inflatable hovercraft available on the market tend to be small, one or two person craft, and apart from the fendering advantages of the tube they are also very portable as the craft can be deflated for stowage or it can be carried on the roof of a car or in a small trailer.

INDEX